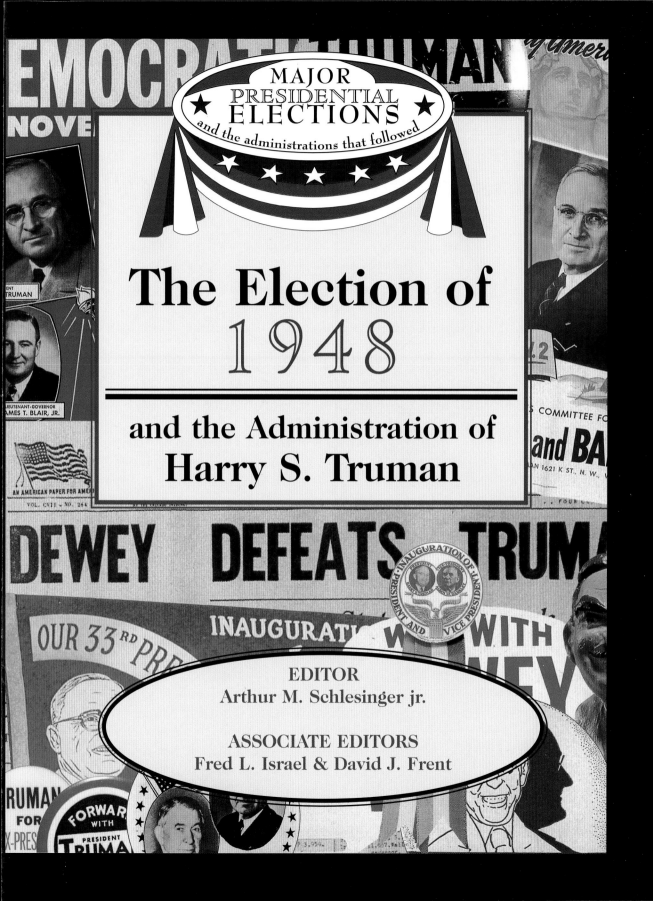

MAJOR PRESIDENTIAL ELECTIONS
and the administrations that followed

The Election of
1948

and the Administration of
Harry S. Truman

EDITOR
Arthur M. Schlesinger jr.

ASSOCIATE EDITORS
Fred L. Israel & David J. Frent

The Elections of 1789 & 1792 and the Administration of George Washington

The Election of 1800 and the Administration of Thomas Jefferson

The Election of 1828 and the Administration of Andrew Jackson

The Election of 1840 and the Harrison/Tyler Administrations

The Election of 1860 and the Administration of Abraham Lincoln

The Election of 1876 and the Administration of Rutherford B. Hayes

The Election of 1896 and the Administration of William McKinley

The Election of 1912 and the Administration of Woodrow Wilson

The Election of 1932 and the Administration of Franklin D. Roosevelt

The Election of 1948 and the Administration of Harry S. Truman

The Election of 1960 and the Administration of John F. Kennedy

The Election of 1968 and the Administration of Richard Nixon

The Election of 1976 and the Administration of Jimmy Carter

The Election of 1980 and the Administration of Ronald Reagan

The Election of 2000 and the Administration of George W. Bush

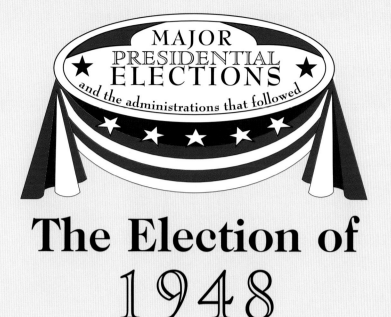

MAJOR PRESIDENTIAL ELECTIONS
and the administrations that followed

The Election of
1948

and the Administration of Harry S. Truman

EDITOR

Arthur M. Schlesinger, jr.
Albert Schweitzer Chair in the Humanities
The City University of New York

★

ASSOCIATE EDITORS

Fred L. Israel
Department of History
The City College of New York

David J. Frent
The David J. and Janice L. Frent
Political Americana Collection

Mason Crest Publishers
Philadelphia

Produced by OTTN Publishing, Stockton, New Jersey

Mason Crest Publishers
370 Reed Road
Broomall PA 19008
www.masoncrest.com

Research Consultant: Patrick R. Hilferty
Editorial Assistant: Jane Ziff

First printing

1 3 5 7 9 8 6 4 2

Library of Congress Cataloging-in-Publication Data

The election of 1948 and the administration of Harry S. Truman / editor, Arthur M. Schlesinger,
Jr.; associate editors, Fred L. Israel & David J. Frent.
    p. cm. — (Major presidential elections and the administrations that followed)
Summary: A discussion of the presidential election of 1948 and the subsequent administration of
Harry S. Truman, based on source documents.
    Includes bibliographical references and index.
    ISBN 1-59084-360-6
1. Presidents—United States—Election—1948—Juvenile literature. 2. Presidents—United
States—Election—1948—Sources—Juvenile literature. 3. Truman, Harry S., 1884-1972—Juvenile
literature. 4. United States—Politics and government—1945-1953—Juvenile literature. 5. United
States—Politics and government—1945-1953—Sources—Juvenile literature. [1. Presidents—
Election—1948—Sources. 2. Truman, Harry S., 1884-1972. 3. Elections. 4. United States—
Politics and government—1945-1953—Sources.]
I. Schlesinger, Arthur Meier, 1917-   II. Israel, Fred L. III. Frent, David J. IV. Series.
E815 .E44 2003
973.918—dc21
                                                                              2002012377

★ Publisher's note: all quotations in this book come
from original sources, and contain the spelling and
grammatical inconsistencies of the original text. ★

Table of Contents

Introduction 6
Arthur M. Schlesinger jr.

The Election of 1948 17
Irwin Ross

Facts at a Glance 34

Truman Becomes President 39

The Atomic Bomb 45

The Truman Doctrine 49

The Marshall Plan 59

Wallace Announces His Candidacy 65

Dewey Accepts the Nomination 71

Truman Accepts the Nomination 77

Platform of the States' Rights Party 87

The Military Is Desegregated 93

Pollster Predicts Dewey Victory 97

Truman's Inaugural Address 103

Statement on Korea, June 26, 1950 113

MacArthur Relieved of Command 115

Court Ruling on Steel Mill Seizure 117

Truman's Farewell Address 121

Further Reading 122

Index 124

★ INTRODUCTION ★
Arthur M. Schlesinger, Jr.

*America suffers from a sort of intermittent fever—what one may call a quintan ague.
Every fourth year there come terrible shakings, passing into the hot fit of the presidential election; then follows what physicians call "the interval"; then again the fit.*

—James Bryce, *The American Commonwealth* (1888)

Running for president is the central rite in the American political order. It was not always so. *Choosing* the chief magistrate had been the point of the quadrennial election from the beginning, but it took a long while for candidates to *run* for the highest office in the land; that is, to solicit, visibly and actively, the support of the voters. These volumes show through text and illustration how those aspiring to the White House have moved on from ascetic self-restraint to shameless self-merchandising. This work thereby illuminates the changing ways the American people have conceived the role of their President. I hope it will also recall to new generations some of the more picturesque and endearing dimensions of American politics.

The primary force behind the revolution in campaign attitudes and techniques was a development unforeseen by the men who framed the Constitution—the rise of the party system. Party competition was not at all their original intent. Quite the contrary: inspired at one or two removes by Lord Bolingbroke's British tract of half a century earlier, *The Idea of a Patriot King*, the Founding Fathers envisaged a Patriot President, standing above party and faction, representing the whole people, offering the nation nonpartisan leadership virtuously dedicated to the common good.

The ideal of the Patriot President was endangered, the Founding Fathers believed, by twin menaces—factionalism and factionalism's ugly offspring, the demagogue. Party competition would only encourage unscrupulous men to appeal to popular passion and prejudice. Alexander Hamilton in the 71st Federalist bemoaned the plight of the people, "beset as they continually are . . . by the snares of the ambitious, the avaricious, the desperate, by the artifices of men who possess their confidence more than they deserve it, and of those who seek to possess rather than to deserve it."

Pervading the Federalist was a theme sounded explicitly both in the first paper and the last: the fear that unleashing popular passions would bring on "the military despotism of a victorious demagogue." If the "mischiefs of faction" were, James Madison admitted in the Tenth Federalist, "sown in the nature of man," the object of politics was to repress this insidious disposition, not to yield to it. "If I could not go to heaven but with a party," said Thomas Jefferson, "I would not go there at all."

So the Father of his Country in his Farewell Address solemnly warned his countrymen against "the baneful effects of the spirit of party." That spirit, Washington conceded, was "inseparable from our nature"; but for popular government it was "truly their worst enemy." The "alternate domination of one faction over another," Washington said, would lead in the end to "formal and permanent despotism." The spirit of a party, "a fire not to be quenched . . . demands a uniform vigilance to prevent its bursting into a flame, lest, instead of warming, it should consume."

Yet even as Washington called on Americans to "discourage and restrain" the spirit of party, parties were beginning to crystallize around him. The eruption of partisanship in defiance of such august counsel argued that party competition might well serve functional necessities in the democratic republic.

After all, honest disagreement over policy and principle called for candid debate. And parties, it appeared, had vital roles to play in the consummation of the Constitution. The distribution of powers among three equal branches inclined the national government toward a chronic condition of stalemate. Parties offered the means of overcoming the constitutional separation of powers by coordinating the executive and legislative branches and furnishing the connective tissue essential to effective government. As national associations, moreover, parties were a force against provincialism and separatism. As instruments of compromise, they encouraged, within the parties as well as between them, the containment and mediation of national quarrels, at least until slavery broke the parties up. Henry D. Thoreau cared little enough for politics, but he saw the point: "Politics is, as it were, the gizzard of society, full of grit and gravel, and the two political parties are its two opposite halves, which grind on each other."

Furthermore, as the illustrations in these volumes so gloriously remind us, party competition was a great source of entertainment and fun—all the more important in those faraway days before the advent of baseball and football, of movies and radio and television. "To take a hand in the regulation of society and to discuss it," Alexis de Tocqueville observed when he visited America in the 1830s, "is his biggest concern and, so to speak, the only pleasure an American knows. . . . Even the women frequently attend public meetings and listen to political harangues as a recreation from their household labors. Debating clubs are, to a certain extent, a substitute for theatrical entertainments."

Condemned by the Founding Fathers, unknown to the Constitution, parties nonetheless imperiously forced themselves into political life. But the party system rose from the bottom up. For half a century, the first half-dozen Presidents continued to hold themselves above party. The disappearance of the Federalist Party after the War of 1812 suspended party competition. James Monroe, with no opponent at all in the election of 1820, presided proudly over the Era of Good Feelings, so called because there were no parties around to excite ill feelings. Monroe's successor, John Quincy Adams, despised electioneering and inveighed against the "fashion of peddling for popularity by traveling around the country gathering crowds together, hawking for public dinners, and spouting empty speeches." Men of the old republic believed presidential candidates should be men who already deserved the people's confidence rather than those seeking to win it. Character and virtue, not charisma and ambition, should be the grounds for choosing a President.

Adams was the last of the old school. Andrew Jackson, by beating him in the 1828 election, legitimized party politics and opened a new political era. The rationale of the new school was provided by Jackson's counselor and successor, Martin Van Buren, the classic philosopher of the role of party in the American democracy. By the time Van Buren took his own oath of office in 1837, parties were entrenched as the instruments of American self-government. In Van Buren's words, party battles "rouse the sluggish to exertion, give increased energy to the most active intellect, excite a salutary vigilance over our public functionaries, and prevent that apathy which has proved the ruin of Republics."

Apathy may indeed have proved the ruin of republics, but rousing the sluggish to exertion proved, ironically, the ruin of Van Buren. The architect of the party system became the first casualty of the razzle-dazzle campaigning the system quickly generated. The Whigs' Tippecanoe-and-Tyler-too campaign of 1840 transmuted the democratic Van Buren into a gilded aristocrat and assured his defeat at the polls. The "peddling for popularity" John Quincy Adams had deplored now became standard for party campaigners.

But the new methods were still forbidden to the presidential candidates themselves. The feeling lingered from earlier days that stumping the country in search of votes was demagoguery beneath the dignity of the presidency. Van Buren's code permitted—indeed expected—parties to inscribe their creed in platforms and candidates to declare their principles in letters published in newspapers. Occasionally candidates—William Henry Harrison in 1840, Winfield Scott in 1852—made a speech, but party surrogates did most of the hard work.

As late as 1858, Van Buren, advising his son John, one of the great popular orators of the time, on the best way to make it to the White House, emphasized the "rule . . . that the people will never make a man President who is so importunate as to show by his life and conversation that he not only has an eye on, but is in active pursuit of the office. . . . No man who has laid himself out for it, and was unwise enough to let the people into his secret, ever yet obtained it. Clay, Calhoun, Webster, Scott, and a host of lesser lights, should serve as a guide-post to future aspirants."

The continuing constraint on personal campaigning by candidates was reinforced by the desire of party managers to present their nominees as all things to all men. In 1835 Nicholas Biddle, the wealthy Philadelphian who had been Jackson's mortal opponent in the famous Bank War, advised the Whigs not to let General Harrison "say one single word about his principles or his creed. . . . Let him say nothing, promise nothing. Let no committee, no convention, no town meeting ever extract from him a single word about what he thinks now, or what he will do hereafter. Let the use of pen and ink be wholly forbidden as if he were a mad poet in Bedlam."

We cherish the memory of the famous debates in 1858 between Abraham Lincoln and Stephen A. Douglas. But those debates were not part of a presidential election. When the presidency was at stake two years later, Lincoln gave no campaign speeches on the issues darkly dividing the country. He even expressed doubt about party platforms—"the formal written platform system," as he called it. The candidate's character and record, Lincoln thought, should constitute his platform: "On just such platforms all our earlier and better Presidents were elected."

However, Douglas, Lincoln's leading opponent in 1860, foreshadowed the future when he broke the sound barrier and dared venture forth on thinly disguised campaign tours. Yet Douglas established no immediate precedent. Indeed, half a dozen years later Lincoln's successor, Andrew Johnson, discredited presidential stumping by his "swing around the circle" in the midterm election of 1866. "His performances in a western tour in advocacy of his own election," commented Benjamin F. Butler, who later led the fight in Congress for Johnson's impeachment, ". . . disgusted everybody." The tenth article of impeachment charged Johnson with bringing "the high office of the President of the United States into contempt, ridicule, and disgrace" by delivering "with a loud voice certain intemperate, inflammatory, and scandalous harangues . . . peculiarly indecent and unbecoming in the Chief Magistrate of the United States."

Though presidential candidates Horatio Seymour in 1868, Rutherford B. Hayes in 1876, and James A. Garfield in 1880 made occasional speeches, only Horace Greeley in 1872, James G. Blaine in 1884, and most spectacularly, William Jennings Bryan in 1896 followed Douglas's audacious example of stumping the country. Such tactics continued to provoke disapproval. Bryan, said John Hay, who had been Lincoln's private secretary and was soon to become McKinley's secretary of state, "is begging for the presidency as a tramp might beg for a pie."

Respectable opinion still preferred the "front porch" campaign, employed by Garfield, by Benjamin Harrison in 1888, and most notably by McKinley in 1896. Here candidates received and addressed numerous delegations at their own homes—a form, as the historian Gil Troy writes, of "stumping in place."

While candidates generally continued to stand on their dignity, popular campaigning in presidential elections flourished in these years, attaining new heights of participation (82 percent of eligible voters in 1876 and never once from 1860 to 1900 under 70 percent) and new wonders of pyrotechnics and ballyhoo. Parties mobilized the electorate as never before, and political iconography was never more ingenious and fantastic. "Politics, considered not as the science of government, but as the art of winning elections and securing office," wrote the keen British observer James Bryce, "has reached in the United States a development surpassing in elaborateness that of England or France as much as the methods of those countries surpass the methods of

Servia or Roumania." Bryce marveled at the "military discipline" of the parties, at "the demonstrations, the parades and receptions, the badges and brass bands and triumphal arches," at the excitement stirred by elections— and at "the disproportion that strikes a European between the merits of the presidential candidate and the blazing enthusiasm which he evokes."

Still the old taboo held back the presidential candidates themselves. Even so irrepressible a campaigner as President Theodore Roosevelt felt obliged to hold his tongue when he ran for reelection in 1904. This unwonted abstinence reminded him, he wrote in considerable frustration, of the July day in 1898 when he was "lying still under shell fire" during the Spanish-American War. "I have continually wished that I could be on the stump myself."

No such constraint inhibited TR, however, when he ran again for the presidency in 1912. Meanwhile, and for the first time, *both* candidates in 1908—Bryan again, and William Howard Taft—actively campaigned for the prize. The duties of the office, on top of the new requirements of campaigning, led Woodrow Wilson to reflect that same year, four years before he himself ran for President, "Men of ordinary physique and discretion cannot be Presidents and live, if the strain be not somehow relieved. We shall be obliged always to be picking our chief magistrates from among wise and prudent athletes,—a small class."

Theodore Roosevelt and Woodrow Wilson combined to legitimate a new conception of presidential candidates as active molders of public opinion in active pursuit of the highest office. Once in the White House, Wilson revived the custom, abandoned by Jefferson, of delivering annual state of the union addresses to Congress in person. In 1916 he became the first incumbent President to stump for his own reelection.

The activist candidate and the bully-pulpit presidency were expressions of the growing democratization of politics. New forms of communication were reconfiguring presidential campaigns. In the nineteenth century the press, far more fiercely partisan then than today, had been the main carrier of political information. In the twentieth century the spread of advertising techniques and the rise of the electronic media—radio, television, computerized public opinion polling—wrought drastic changes in the methodology of politics. In particular the electronic age diminished and now threatens to dissolve the historic role of the party.

The old system had three tiers: the politician at one end; the voter at the other; and the party in between. The party's function was to negotiate between the politician and the voters, interpreting each to the other and providing the link that held the political process together. The electric revolution has substantially abolished the sovereignty of the party. Where once the voter turned to the local party leader to find out whom to support, now he looks at television and makes up his own mind. Where once the politician turned to the local party leader to find out what people are thinking, he now takes a computerized poll.

The electronic era has created a new breed of professional consultants, "handlers," who by the 1980s had taken control of campaigns away from the politicians. The traditional pageantry—rallies, torchlight processions, volunteers, leaflets, billboards, bumper stickers—is now largely a thing of the past. Television replaces the party as the means of mobilizing the voter. And as the party is left to wither on the vine, the presidential candidate becomes more pivotal than ever. We shall see the rise of personalist movements, founded not on historic organizations but on compelling personalities, private fortunes, and popular frustrations. Without the stabilizing influence of parties, American politics would grow angrier, wilder, and more irresponsible.

Things have changed considerably from the austerities of the old republic. Where once voters preferred to call presumably reluctant candidates to the duties of the supreme magistracy and rejected pursuit of the office as evidence of dangerous ambition, now they expect candidates to come to them, explain their views and plead for their support. Where nonpartisan virtue had been the essence, now candidates must prove to voters that they have the requisite "fire in the belly." "'Twud be inth'restin," said Mr. Dooley, ". . . if th' fathers iv th' counthry cud come back an' see what has happened while they've been away. In times past whin ye voted f'r prisident ye didn't vote f'r a man. Ye voted f'r a kind iv a statue that ye'd put up in ye'er own mind on a marble pidistal. Ye nivir heerd iv George Wash'nton goin' around th' counthry distributin' five cint see-gars."

We have reversed the original notion that ambition must be disguised and the office seek the man. Now the man—and soon, one must hope, the woman— seeks the office and does so without guilt or shame or inhibition. This is not necessarily a degradation of democracy. Dropping the disguise is a gain for candor, and personal avowals of convictions and policies may elevate and educate the electorate.

On the other hand, the electronic era has dismally reduced both the intellectual content of campaigns and the attention span of audiences. In the nineteenth century political speeches lasted for a couple of hours and dealt with issues in systematic and exhaustive fashion. Voters drove wagons for miles to hear Webster and Clay, Bryan and Teddy Roosevelt, and felt cheated if the famous orator did not give them their money's worth. Then radio came along and cut political addresses down first to an hour, soon to thirty minutes—still enough time to develop substantive arguments.

But television has shrunk the political talk first to fifteen minutes, now to the sound bite and the thirty-second spot. Advertising agencies today sell candidates with all the cynical contrivance they previously devoted to selling detergents and mouthwash. The result is the debasement of American politics. "The idea that you can merchandise candidates for high office like breakfast cereal," Adlai Stevenson said in 1952, "is the ultimate indignity to the democratic process."

Still Bryce's "intermittent fever" will be upon us every fourth year. We will continue to watch wise if not always prudent athletes in their sprint for the White House, enjoy the quadrennial spectacle and agonize about the outcome.

"The strife of the election," said Lincoln after his reelection in 1864, "is but human-nature practically applied to the facts. What has occurred in this case, must ever recur in similar cases. Human-nature will not change."

Lincoln, as usual, was right. Despite the transformation in political methods there remains a basic continuity in political emotions. "For a long while before the appointed time has come," Tocqueville wrote more than a century and a half ago, "the election becomes the important and, so to speak, the all-engrossing topic of discussion. Factional ardor is redoubled, and all the artificial passions which the imagination can create in a happy and peaceful land are agitated and brought to light. . . .

"As the election draws near, the activity of intrigue and the agitation of the populace increase; the citizens are divided into hostile camps, each of which assumes the name of its favorite candidate; the whole nation glows with feverish excitement; the election is the daily theme of the press, the subject of every private conversation, the end of every thought and every action, the sole interest of the present.

"It is true," Tocqueville added, "that as soon as the choice is determined, this ardor is dispelled, calm returns, and the river, which had nearly broken its banks, sinks to its usual level; but who can refrain from astonishment that such a storm should have arisen?"

The election storm in the end blows fresh and clean. With the tragic exception of 1860, the American people have invariably accepted the result and given the victor their hopes and blessings. For all its flaws and follies, democracy abides.

Let us now turn the pages and watch the gaudy parade of American presidential politics pass by in all its careless glory.

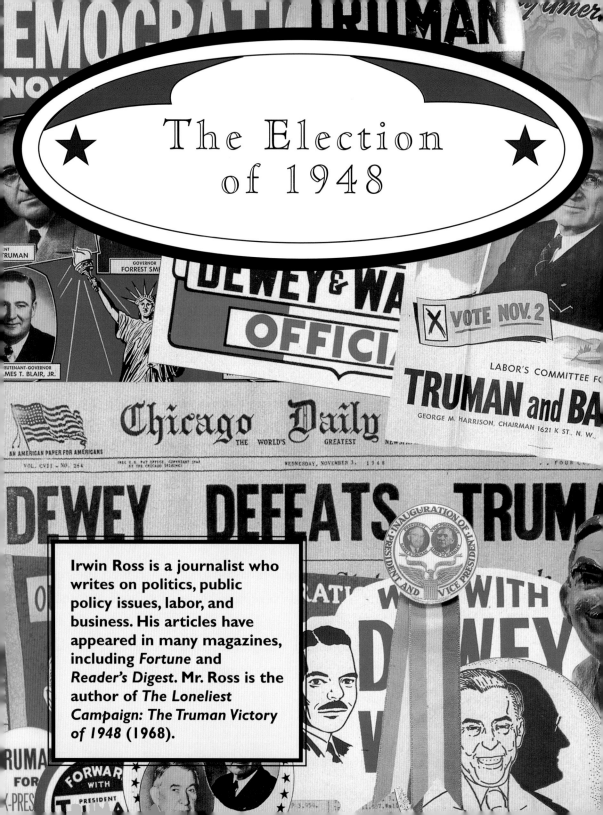

The Election
of 1948

Irwin Ross is a journalist who
writes on politics, public
policy issues, labor, and
business. His articles have
appeared in many magazines,
including *Fortune* and
Reader's Digest. Mr. Ross is the
author of *The Loneliest
Campaign: The Truman Victory
of 1948* (1968).

Perhaps the most vivid memory of the 1948 presidential election for anyone who lived through it is of a triumphant President Harry Truman holding aloft the front page of the *Chicago Tribune* with the banner headline DEWEY DEFEATS TRUMAN. It was the *Tribune*'s first edition, of course, which went to press long before the final returns next morning upended all forecasts. But the 1948 election was notable not only for one of the most startling upsets in American presidential politics but for a sophistication of campaign management and tactics that, oddly, was not apparent at the time.

What was apparent was in many ways a dull campaign in which a beleaguered incumbent went barnstorming around the country, hurling invective at the opposition party and especially at the national Congress which it controlled, while the challenger, Governor Thomas E. Dewey of New York, took so elevated a high road that at times he seemed not to be participating in the same campaign. To be sure, there were many lively moments along the way, mostly contributed by Truman, but the campaign basically seemed dull because it never possessed any of the qualities of a horse race.

From the outset, it was clear to almost all observers that Dewey was destined to win. Truman was neither a dynamic leader nor a brilliant speaker; in his first year or two he presided over the country without providing any clear sense of direction, except in foreign policy; at times he seemed incompetent, and sometimes downright silly. So certain were Democratic leaders that Truman was doomed to defeat that many, in the spring of 1948, sought to dump him and nominate General Dwight D. Eisenhower—whose party affiliation was not known. But the general would not play. Truman was finally nominated at the Democratic convention in July pretty much *faute de mieux*.

Early in August the Gallup poll showed Truman trailing Dewey 37 percent to 48 percent; some days later the Roper poll gave Truman a mere 31.5 percent of the vote. Not only did later polls always place Dewey in the lead but Truman had also suffered two defections that seemed insurmountable. Former Vice President Henry Wallace led a left-wing exodus that created the Progressive Party, with himself as its presidential nominee, while a large group of rebellious southern segregationists created the States' Rights Party, which nominated Governor J. Strom Thurmond of South Carolina for president. The Dixiecrats were expected to take several states in the South, whereas Wallace was thought to be sufficiently popular in the Northeast, California, and sections of the Midwest to throw a handful of states to Dewey.

Not only was the outlook dismal, but the Truman campaign seemed both improvised and disorganized. Yet there was both method and long-range strategy behind the President's effort, though few if any outsiders realized it. Campaign planning had actually begun in the summer of 1947. The key strategy document was the now famous Clifford memorandum, presented to the President in November by Clark Clifford, the White House counsel. For many years Clifford got sole credit for this prescient paper, but he tells us in his memoirs, published in 1991, that it was based on a memorandum prepared by James Rowe,

Neckties for three of the 1948 candidates—Thomas Dewey, Harry S. Truman, and Henry Wallace.

who had formerly served as an assistant to Roosevelt. Truman thought so highly of the Clifford paper that he kept it in a desk drawer throughout the campaign.

It was indeed a remarkable piece of forecasting and analysis. Clifford stated flatly that Dewey would be the Republican candidate and that Wallace would run on a third-party ticket, neither of which were certainties at that early stage. He asserted that there would be no southern breakaway—the one major error in the forecast. He correctly anticipated that the Wallace defection would cost Truman several states, but argued that the President could still win:

> If the Democrats carry the solid South and also those Western States carried in 1944, they will have 216 of the required 266 electoral votes. And if the Democratic Party is powerful enough to capture the West, it will almost certainly pick up enough of the doubtful Middle Western and Eastern states to get 50 more votes. . . . We could lose New York, Pennsylvania, Illinois, New Jersey, Ohio, Massachusetts—all the "big" states and still win.

To achieve all that, Clifford argued that Truman had to adopt an unabashedly liberal line on economic issues, appealing to all the elements of the old Roosevelt coalition of labor, the farmers, Negroes in the North, middle-class liberals, as well as the South, whose voters were then predominantly white. (In the end, Truman did take the bulk of the South, despite the loss of four states.) Clifford thought the farmers were safe for Truman, but stressed the importance of heavy labor-union participation. There was no danger of labor going Republican, but it could stay home as it did in 1946, causing the Democrats to lose the Congress.

Cardboard sign. Reference is to Lyndon Johnson's narrow and controversial victory in the 1948 Texas Democratic senatorial primary.

Cardboard poster for Wallace and Taylor. Henry Wallace, Truman's secretary of commerce, broke with the president over his Cold War policies. In December 1947 he announced he would run for president on a third-party ticket.

Clifford also urged that the President start his reelection effort with his state of the union message in January, and the event that offered him an unparalleled opportunity to broadcast his themes to the nation above the heads of a hostile Congress. He should announce his maximum program, for there was no chance of getting anything passed and hence no need for moderation or attempts at compromise. The speech was scheduled for January 7, 1948, and for maximum impact Truman agreed to deliver it in person, which was by no means routine in those years. There was no TV coverage but it was carried by radio. And it was hard-hitting. Truman called for an aggressive anti-inflation program (a rapidly rising price level had been a major issue throughout 1947), a generous federal housing program, increases in the minimum wage, unemployment compensation and Social Security benefits, wide-ranging civil rights legislation, a program of national medical insurance, more dams and reclamation projects, and continual price supports, of course, for the farmer. By the time he finished,

Truman had articulated a full-blown welfare state, which was not completed until the Johnson administration—apart from national health insurance.

After the program was announced, the White House never let up. Week after week, Truman sent messages to the Congress, each urging the adoption of specific items on his agenda. The civil rights message—so important to retaining the loyalty of black voters—came in February. For his pains, Truman was met with indifference and ridicule, but was his goal to dramatize congressional inaction. Week after week, he was accumulating ammunition for his campaign assaults on the "do-nothing" Eightieth Congress.

A further step in this strategy came in the early hours of July 15 when Truman ended his acceptance speech before the Democratic convention by announcing that he was calling the Eightieth Congress back into session on July 26 in order to enact various pressing items of domestic legislation, some of which had been favored in the Republican platform adopted three weeks before. "If there is any reality behind the Republican Party

After the Democratic National Convention, a group of southern Democrats who rejected the civil-rights plank in the Democratic platform broke away from the party. They formed their own party, the States' Rights Party, and nominated South Carolina Governor J. Strom Thurmond for president and Mississippi Governor Fielding Wright of Mississippi for vice president.

GOV. J. STROM THURMOND
FOR PRESIDENT

STATES' RIGHTS

SHIELD OF YOUR LIBERTY

GOV. FIELDING L. WRIGHT
FOR VICE-PRESIDENT

STATES' RIGHTS DEMOCRATS

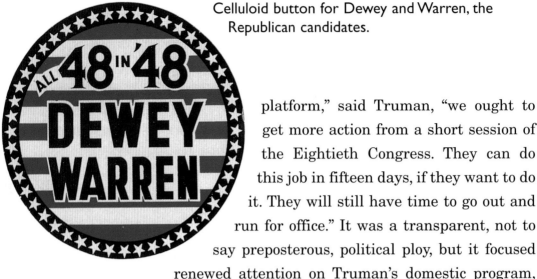

Celluloid button for Dewey and Warren, the Republican candidates.

platform," said Truman, "we ought to get more action from a short session of the Eightieth Congress. They can do this job in fifteen days, if they want to do it. They will still have time to go out and run for office." It was a transparent, not to say preposterous, political ploy, but it focused renewed attention on Truman's domestic program, and it put the Republicans on the spot. Truman again journeyed to the Hill to deliver his proposals, and he was again scorned.

Meantime, Dewey and his advisers devised a campaign that assumed victory and was designed to avoid any mishaps or intemperate responses as well as any specific commitments that might embarrass him after he took office. This was not a nonsensical approach (although it did not excuse the dullness of his speeches), given the unanimity of expert opinion that he was certain to win, a conviction that was reinforced every fortnight or so when another set of opinion polls came out.

Campaign techniques, style, and rhetoric flowed naturally from the candidates' divergent strategies. This was the last of the pre-television campaigns; though the conventions were televised, so few homes had sets that politicians could be indifferent to the camera eye. It was also the last of the major whistle-stop campaigns, though some use of campaign trains occurred in 1952 and occasionally later. In 1948, however, there were only two ways of reaching the electorate directly—radio speeches and public rallies. Newspaper accounts of what the candidates said were fairly comprehensive—and there were of course far more newspapers—but national

radio news broadcasts were limited to fifteen minutes and provided no opportunity for "sound bites," a term that was decades away from being invented.

Both Truman and Dewey campaigned extensively by rail, criss-crossing the country and living on their trains with a large entourage of staff and press. The standard format provided several short back-platform appearances each day, culminating in a large rally for several thousand in a hall. The Republicans were also able to afford a campaign train for their vice-presidential candidate, Governor Earl Warren, but the Democratic candidate, Senator Alben Barkley, had to content himself with a chartered plane, as did Henry Wallace. No presidential candidate ever devoted himself more energetically to whistle-stop campaigning than Harry Truman. He sometimes spoke a dozen times a day. On

Kentucky Democratic Party poster. There is an abundant variety of paper items from the 1948 campaign.

the first full day of his September tour, he addressed his first crowd at 5:45 A.M. in Rock Island, Illinois, and made his final appeal at 8:10 P.M. in Polo, Missouri, confiding to the audience that "I didn't think I was going to be able to do it but the railroad finally consented to stop."

Truman was effective as a back-platform campaigner because he had finally mastered the art of ad-libbing. For three years, he had been the despair of his advisers, for he was incapable of reading a text with pace or emphasis, not to speak of dramatic flourish or passion. In a word, he droned. Finally, in April 1948, he was prevailed upon by his handlers to try an experiment. After a prepared speech before the American Society of Newspaper Editors in Washington, he launched into an extemporaneous talk about American relations with the Soviet Union. He was informal, relaxed, and surprisingly lively—in sync with the audience as he usually was when speaking to a small group in the White House. He was not quite speaking off the top of his head, for he had notes prepared by his staff that outlined the topics to be covered.

So well received were these off-the-cuff remarks and a few similar exercises in Washington that Truman continued his improvisations on his so-called "non-political" tour in June. The excuse for the trip was Truman's acceptance of an invitation to deliver a commencement address at the University of California in Berkeley. Truman could have flown, of course, but instead he aped Roosevelt's wartime precedent of an "inspection tour." It was an elaborate operation, involving a sixteen-car train and a journey to eighteen states. The opposition was understandably outraged, but, as always, helpless to prevent a President from managing the news by creating an event.

The June trip was really the start of Truman's public campaign. Advance work for the trip was poor and there were many snafus, but Truman became quite accomplished at the back-platform ad-lib and he was wowing the crowds. By September, his performance followed a standard pattern, aided by an outline from which

Lithographed tin button for Truman. The president's civil rights program was the most controversial feature of his Fair Deal.

Republican 1948 campaign items. (Right) cardboard poster praising Dewey's achievements as governor of New York. (Below) Republican campaign buttons featured caricatures of jackasses to help form slogans.

GET YOUR 🫏 OFF THE GRASS! IT'S DEWEY

DEWEY GETS THINGS DONE!

LOOK WHAT DEWEY DID!

Personal Income Tax cut 40%

One of Governor Dewey's most phenomenal contributions to good government has been his sound fiscal policy. He has been able to cut taxes, build up surpluses, and at the same time render state services that make New York government the most progressive in history. Personal income tax was cut 40% and business income taxes were cut 25%.

Surplus built up of $673,000,000

A $673,000,000 surplus was built up in four years and put aside for post-war construction and tax stabilization reserves. State aid to local governments has been increased by almost two-thirds under Governor Dewey.

Taxpayers' savings $800,000,000

Under Governor Dewey, taxpayers saved this sum through reduction of regular state taxes, mostly since the war.

$400,000,000 Veterans' Bonus Paid

And by two-year financing—instead of the usual forty years—taxpayers will save $140,000,000 on interest.

Housing for 160,000 persons

The Dewey program now under way—36 public housing projects—will provide homes for almost 160,000 persons otherwise doomed to unsafe, unsanitary places. Veteran housing is in addition to this. New York leads the nation in slum clearance and public housing for families of low income.

State debt reduced 27% in 4 years

In four years under Governor Dewey, New York State has reduced its debt by $136,000,000 or 27%. Dewey believes in pay-as-you-go.

140,000 new small businesses established

A special campaign to aid small business resulted in an increase of 130,000 in the number of business firms in the state since V-J Day. Governor Dewey set up a program of individual assistance to small businessmen and to men and women starting a business of their own.

VOTE DEWEY-WARREN

he took off. He generally began with an appropriate local reference, never forgot a plug for a local Democratic candidate, and concentrated on a single main subject that involved the immediate economic interests of his listeners—jobs, inflation, the housing crunch, the shortage of grain storage bins in the farm belt, dams and reclamation projects in the West, and so on.

Truman would contrast the Democrats and Republicans in the starkest populist terms—the party of the people against the party of the rich. No old-fashioned socialist orator could have put more of a class spin on Truman's rhetoric. In his first major speech of the September tour, at the National Plowing Contest in Dexter, Iowa, he denounced "Wall Street reactionaries" and "gluttons of privilege" as well as the Republican Congress, which he charged had "stuck a pitchfork" in the farmer's back. Truman was relentless:

> I wonder how many times you have to be hit on the head before you find out who's hitting you . . . these Republican gluttons of privilege are cold men. They are cunning men . . . what they have taken away from you thus far would only be an appetizer for the economic tapeworm of big business.

Truman's extravagant assaults never provoked Dewey to an angry retort, even when late in the campaign the President linked the threat of fascism to a Republican victory. In a speech in Chicago on October 25, Truman first inveighed against "the powerful reactionary forces which are silently undermining our democratic institutions." He warned that "when a few men get control of the economy of a nation, they find a 'front man' to

These buttons refer to Dewey's September-October train tour. The lower button is attached to a plastic train-shaped whistle.

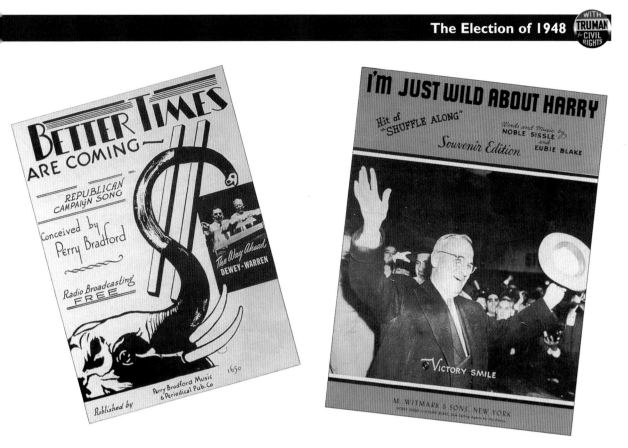

Sheet music for Dewey and Truman, including Eubie Blake's "I'm Just Wild about Harry," which became Truman's theme song.

run the country for them." Thus, in Germany, "they put money and influence behind Adolf Hitler. We know the rest of the story." Similarly in Italy. "PRESIDENT LIKENS DEWEY TO HITLER AS FASCISTS' TOOL," reported the *New York Times* the next day.

But Dewey would not take the bait. The last thing he wanted was a slanging match with Harry. Dewey made occasional slighting references to the failings of the Democratic administration, and he sometimes defended the Eightieth Congress, but never in ringing terms. He had obviously made the shrewd political decision not to let his opponent set the campaign agenda. The result was that there was no long-distance debate of the issues, no thrust and counterthrust to enliven the headlines.

Selection of paper items from the 1948 election.

Dewey's entire campaign had an air of relaxation. While Truman had been campaigning since June, Dewey only began his first train tour on September 19, two days after Truman set out from Washington. Nor did Dewey exert himself as much. He made half as many back-platform appearances as Truman and, unlike Truman, always delivered the same set speech, apart from local references and perhaps a paragraph or two

Celluloid button for Truman.

from his main speech scheduled for that evening. At times he seemed to be exerting himself more on behalf of candidates for the House and Senate, many of whom were thought to be in trouble, than his own cause. He had no desire as president to confront a Democratic Congress.

From the outset, Dewey's tour of the country struck a tone of moral high mindedness from which he rarely deviated. His first major speech of the September tour, in Dexter, Iowa, was characteristically entitled "The Challenge of Tomorrow." In his rich, mellifluous baritone, he told the nation that

> Tonight we enter upon a campaign to unite America. On January 20, we will enter upon a new era. We propose to install in Washington an administration which has faith in the American people, a warm understanding of their needs and the competence to meet them. We will rediscover the essential unity of our people and the spiritual strength which makes our country great. We will begin to move forward again shoulder to shoulder toward an even greater America and a better life for every American, in the nation working effectively for the peace of the world.

At times Dewey put a bit more bite into his message—as when he continually promised that come January 20 Washington would witness "the biggest unraveling, unsnarling, untangling operation in our nation's history"—but he never failed to give the impression that he was engaged not in a political campaign but in a stately coronation march. His composure deserted him only once, in a famous incident in Beaucoup, Illinois. As Dewey started to speak from the rear of the train, it rolled backward into

Pennants for Truman and Dewey.

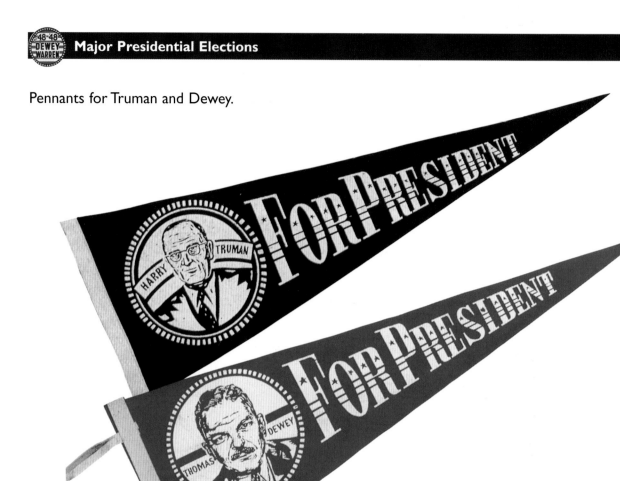

the crowd. No one was hurt but Dewey exploded, "That's the first lunatic I've had for an engineer! He probably ought to be shot at sunrise, but I guess we can let him off because no one was hurt." The Democrats kept recalling Dewey's crack to the end of the campaign, charging that he was hostile to working folk.

The words of both candidates were available to millions of their countrymen via radio, but Dewey's oratory could be more readily tuned in, for the Republicans had more money available to buy time. Throughout the campaign, the Democrats were strapped for funds. The networks were often so concerned about the party's poverty that they demanded payment in advance. On occasion the national committee could not get the money in enough time to channel it through a bank account and the committee chairman, Senator J. Howard McGrath, would hasten to the studio with $25,000 or $30,000 in cash. It would be just enough to pay for the stipulated time and Truman was sometimes cut off the air when he ran over.

Perhaps more important to campaign managers than radio exposure was corralling the populace to see and hear the candidates. This was still the era of the large campaign rally, in auditoriums, open-air stadiums and even the street. In New York City, for example, no self-respecting campaign could come to an end without a rally in Madison Square Garden. In 1948, the Garden was populated not only by the Democrats and Republicans but by the Progressives, who attracted 19,000 to Truman's 16,000. With television not a factor, there was no fear, as in recent campaigns, of organized heckling that would make a shambles of a show that was being produced largely for an unseen audience. Crowds were important not only in the halls but in the streets, along the line of the motorcade. This was also still an era of relative innocence, before the ever-present fear of assassination, and so the routes of motorcades were widely publicized, with the candidates on display. Not only did these processions help stimulate voter enthusiasm, or so it was thought, but the size of the crowds was taken as an indication of a campaign's relative success.

Throughout the campaign, Truman attracted large throngs, with more and more people emerging in the final days. In mid-October, 100,000 people in Akron, Ohio, watched his motorcade; 50,000 came out in Dayton. Huge throngs showed up in the small cities of Indiana—25,000 in Kokomo, 20,000 in Hammond, 12,000 in Logansport. In Chicago, in the final weeks of the campaign, 50,000 people paraded through the downtown streets to the Chicago Stadium and an estimated 500,000 watched on the sidelines.

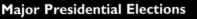

Chicago Daily Tribune

THE WORLD'S GREATEST NEWSPAPER

HOME

VOL. CVII — NO. 264   WEDNESDAY, NOVEMBER 3, 1948   FOUR CENTS·PAY NO MORE

DEWEY DEFEATS TRUMAN

G.O.P. Sweep Indicated in State; Boyle Leads in City

REPUBLICAN TICKET AHEAD OF 1944 VOTE

Tops Coghlan in Hot Race for Attorney

RECORD CITY VOTE SEEN IN LATE TALLIES

BULLETINS ON ELECTIONS

Early Count Gives G.O.P. Senate Edge

PUTS G.O.P. BACK IN THE WHITE HOUSE

Town Balloting Gives Trend

Suburban Ballot Near 375,000

COOK COUNTY

NATION

Sizable Electoral Margin Seen

THE WEATHER

CHICAGO AND VICINITY: Partly cloudy.

In Boston the street crowds were estimated at 250,000. All this was duly chronicled in the papers, but its significance was discounted. Journalists tended to attribute Truman's drawing power to curiosity, little more. Meantime, from mid-October Dewey was pulling fewer people into the streets, a fact that was again noted but not regarded as significant.

The final polls showed a decline in Dewey's support, but still a substantial lead. Gallup gave Dewey 49.5 percent of the vote to 44.5 percent for Truman; Crossley produced almost the same numbers—49.9 percent to 44.8 percent. The experts were thus confirmed in their views. What they did not realize was that the pollsters had stopped interviewing much too soon. The Gallup poll published on the eve of the election was derived from two national samples taken in mid-October. Thus Gallup, like Crossley and Roper (who had stopped polling in September), could not pick up last-minute switches as well as the late decisions of previously undecided voters; the net effect of both favored Truman and helped him get 2 million more votes than Dewey—49.5 percent as against 45 percent for Dewey and 2.4 percent each for Thurmond and Wallace—and a top-heavy majority— 303 to 189 with 39 for Thurmond—in the electoral college. Clearly those crowds in late October were voting with their feet before they got into the polling booth.

Opposite: perhaps the most famous newspaper headline in American history, *Chicago Daily Tribune*, November 3, 1948.

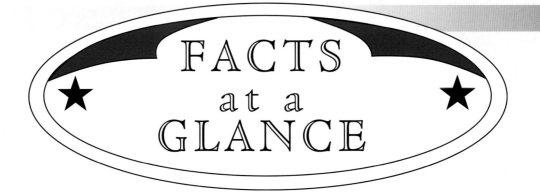

HARRY S. TRUMAN

- **Born:** May 8, 1884, in Lamar, Missouri
- **Parents:** John and Martha Ellen Young Truman
- **Education:** Attended the University of Kansas City Law School
- **Occupation:** farmer, public official
- **Married:** Elizabeth "Bess" Wallace (1885–1982) on June 28, 1919
- **Children:** Mary Margaret Truman (1924–   )
- **Died:** December 26, 1972, in Kansas City, Missouri

Served as the 33RD PRESIDENT OF THE UNITED STATES,

- April 12, 1945, to January 20, 1953

VICE PRESIDENT

- Alben W. Barkley (1949–53)

OTHER POLITICAL POSITIONS

- Judge, Jackson County, Missouri, 1922–24, 1926–34
- United States Senator, 1935–45
- Vice President of the United States, 1945

CABINET

Secretary of State
- Edward R. Stettinius, Jr. (1945)
- James F. Byrnes (1945–47)
- George C. Marshall (1947–49)
- Dean G. Acheson (1949–53)

Secretary of the Treasury
- Henry Morgenthau, Jr. (1945)
- Frederick M. Vinson (1945–46)
- John W. Snyder (1946–53)

Secretary of War
- Henry L. Stimson (1945)
- Robert P. Patterson (1945–47)
- Kenneth C. Royall (1947)

Secretary of Defense
- James V. Forrestal (1947–49)
- Louis A. Johnson (1949–50)
- George C. Marshall (1950–51)
- Robert A. Lovett (1951–53)

Attorney General
- Francis B. Biddle (1945)
- Thomas C. Clark (1945–49)
- J. Howard McGrath (1949–52)

Postmaster General
- Frank C. Walker (1945)
- Robert E. Hannegan (1945–47)
- Jesse M. Donaldson (1947–53)

Secretary of the Navy
- James V. Forrestal (1945–47)

Secretary of the Interior
- Harold L. Ickes (1945–46)
- Julius A. Krug (1946–49)
- Oscar L. Chapman (1950–53)

Secretary of Agriculture
- Claude R. Wickard (1945)
- Clinton P. Anderson (1945–48)
- Charles F. Brannan (1948–53)

Secretary of Commerce
- Henry A. Wallace (1945–46)
- William A. Harriman (1946–48)
- Charles Sawyer (1948–53)

Secretary of Labor
- Frances Perkins (1945)
- Lewis B. Schwellenbach (1945–48)
- Maurice J. Tobin (1949–53)

NOTABLE EVENTS DURING TRUMAN'S ADMINISTRATION

1945 Harry S. Truman is sworn in as the 33rd president of the United States on April 12, after the death of Franklin D. Roosevelt; on August 6 the United States drops the first atomic bomb on Hiroshima. A second bomb is dropped on Nagasaki three days later. Japan surrenders, ending World War II.

1947 On March 12, Truman requests $400 million to halt the spread of communism in Greece and Turkey (the Truman Doctrine); in June, the Taft-Hartley Bill (Labor-Management Relations Act of 1947) is passed by Congress over the president's veto.

1948 In February, Truman asks Congress for civil rights legislation; On April 3, the U.S. begins to provide financial assistance to European countries under what becomes known as the Marshall Plan; on May 14, the United States recognizes the new state of Israel; in June, the Berlin airlift begins in response to a Russian blockade of that occupied German city; on November 2, Truman is elected to a second term as president.

1949 Truman presents his legislative program to Congress (known as the Fair Deal) during the State of the Union message January 5; in August, the North Atlantic Treaty Organization (NATO) is created.

1950 In June, the American military is sent to help South Korean troops in resisting an invasion by communist North Korea; on November 1, an attempt by two Puerto Rican nationalists to assassinate Truman fails; in December, Communist China becomes involved in the Korean conflict.

1951 On April 11, Truman dismisses General Douglas MacArthur as commander of American and United Nations forces in Korea.

1952 On April 8, Truman signs an executive order directing the Secretary of Commerce to seize steel mills to prevent a strike by steel workers. Seven weeks later the Supreme Court declares this order unconstitutional.

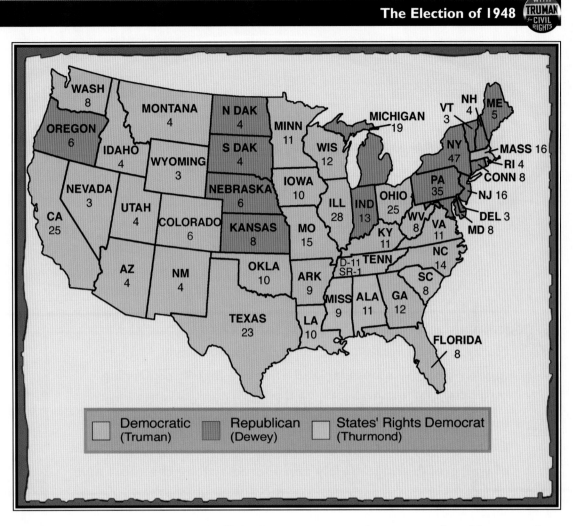

Democratic (Truman) Republican (Dewey) States' Rights Democrat (Thurmond)

In 1948 Harry S. Truman pulled off the biggest upset in American political history when he defeated Thomas Dewey. The incumbent president (who had assumed office upon the death of Franklin D. Roosevelt three years earlier) received 49.5 percent of the popular vote to Dewey's 45.1 percent. Truman's margin was much greater in the electoral college (303 to 189 for Dewey). Both the States' Rights candidate, J. Strom Thurmond, and Progressive Party candidate, Henry Wallace, won more than 1.1 million votes (each receiving about 2.4 percent of the national total) with Thurmond receiving electoral votes (39) from five southern states.

Truman Becomes President

Harry Truman was elected to the U. S. Senate in 1934. He quickly became a popular and effective legislator. During World War II, he chaired a special Senate committee to investigate problems of defense production. The Truman Committee, as it was popularly known, exposed the excesses of war profiteering. Widely considered among the most able of senators and acceptable to all factions of the Democratic Party, Truman was the compromise choice for vice president in 1944. His selection by the party leaders was made without his knowledge but he accepted when told that he was Franklin Roosevelt's choice. In November 1944, Roosevelt and Truman were elected without any difficulty. Five months later on April 12, 1945, Roosevelt died of a stroke.

"When they told me yesterday what had happened," Harry Truman told reporters the day after Roosevelt's death, "I felt like the moon, the stars and all the planets fell on me." On April 16, Truman addressed a joint session of Congress. He pledged to continue Roosevelt's policies.

It is with a heavy heart that I stand before you, my friends and colleagues, in the Congress of the United States.

Only yesterday, we laid to rest the mortal remains of our beloved President, Franklin Delano Roosevelt. At a time like this, words are inadequate. The most eloquent tribute would be a reverent silence.

Yet, in this decisive hour, when world events are moving so rapidly, our silence might be misunderstood and might give comfort to our enemies.

In His infinite wisdom, Almighty God has seen fit to take from us a great man who loved, and was beloved by, all humanity.

No man could possibly fill the tremendous void left by the passing of that noble soul. No words can ease the aching hearts of untold millions of every race, creed, and color. The world knows it has lost a heroic champion of justice and freedom.

Tragic fate has thrust upon us grave responsibilities. We *must* carry on. Our departed leader never looked backward. He looked forward and moved forward. That is what he would want us to do. That is what America *will* do.

So much blood has already been shed for the ideals which we cherish, and for which Franklin Delano Roosevelt lived and died, that we dare not permit even a momentary pause in the hard fight for victory.

Today, the entire world is looking to America for enlightened leadership to peace and progress. Such a leadership requires vision, courage, and tolerance. It can be provided only by a united nation deeply devoted to the highest ideals.

With great humility I call upon all Americans to help me keep our nation united in defense of those ideals which have been so eloquently proclaimed by Franklin Roosevelt.

I want in turn to assure my fellow Americans and all of those who love peace and liberty throughout the world that I will support and defend those ideals with all my strength and all my heart. That is my duty and I shall not shirk it.

So that there can be no possible misunderstanding, both Germany and Japan can be certain, beyond any shadow of a doubt, that America will continue the fight for freedom until no vestige of resistance remains!

We are deeply conscious of the fact that much hard fighting is still ahead of us. Having to pay such a heavy price to make complete victory certain, America will never become a party to any plan for partial victory!

To settle for merely another temporary respite would surely jeopardize the future security of all the world.

Our demand has been—and it *remains*—unconditional surrender! We will not traffic with the breakers of the peace on the terms of the peace.

The responsibility for making of the peace—and it is a very grave responsibility—must rest with the defenders of the peace. We are not unconscious of the dictates of humanity. We do not wish to see unnecessary or unjustified suffering. But the laws of God and of man have been violated and the guilty must not go unpunished. Nothing shall shake our determination to punish the war criminals even though we must pursue them to the ends of the earth.

Lasting peace can never be secured if we permit our dangerous opponents to plot future wars with impunity at any mountain retreat-however distant.

In this shrinking world, it is futile to seek safety behind geographical barriers. Real security will be found only in law and in justice.

Here in America, we have labored long and hard to achieve a social order worthy of our great heritage. In our time, tremendous progress has been made toward a really democratic way of life. Let me assure the forward-looking people of America that there will be no relaxation in our efforts to improve the lot of the common people.

In the difficult days ahead, unquestionably we shall face problems of staggering proportions. However, with the faith of our fathers in our hearts, we do not fear the future.

On the battlefields, we have frequently faced overwhelming odds—and won! At home, Americans will not be less resolute!

We shall never cease our struggle to preserve and maintain our American way of life.

At this moment, America, along with her brave Allies, is paying again a heavy price for the defense of our freedom. With characteristic energy, we are assisting in the liberation of entire nations. Gradually, the shackles of slavery are being broken by the forces of freedom.

All of us are praying for a speedy victory. Every day peace is delayed costs a terrible toll.

The armies of liberation today are bringing to an end Hitler's ghastly threat to dominate the world. Tokyo rocks under the weight of our bombs. [. . .]

Our debt to the heroic men and valiant women in the service of our country can never be repaid. They have earned our undying gratitude. America will never forget their sacrifices. Because of these sacrifices, the dawn of justice and freedom throughout the world slowly casts its gleam across the horizon.

Our forefathers came to our rugged shores in search of religious tolerance, political freedom and economic opportunity. For those fundamental rights, they risked their lives. We well know today that such rights can be preserved only by constant vigilance, the eternal price of liberty!

Within an hour after I took the oath of office, I announced that the San Francisco Conference would proceed. We will face the problems of peace with the same courage that we have faced and mastered the problems of war.

In the memory of those who have made the supreme sacrifice—in the memory of our fallen President—*we shall not fail*!

It is not enough to yearn for peace. We must work, and if necessary, fight for it. The task of creating a sound international organization is complicated and difficult. Yet, without such organization, the rights of man on earth cannot be protected. Machinery for the just settlement of international differences must be found. Without such machinery, the entire world will have to remain an armed camp. The world will be doomed to deadly conflict, devoid of hope for real peace.

Fortunately, people have retained hope for a durable peace. Thoughtful people have always had faith that ultimately justice *must* triumph. Past experience surely indicates that, without justice, an enduring peace becomes impossible.

In bitter despair, some people have come to believe that wars are inevitable. With tragic fatalism, they insist that wars have always been, of necessity, and of necessity wars always will be. To such defeatism, men and women of good will must not and can not yield. The outlook for humanity is not so hopeless. [. . .] Aggressors could not dominate the human mind. As long as hope remains, the spirit of man will *never* be crushed.

But hope alone was not and is not sufficient to avert war. We must not only have hope but we must have faith enough to work with other peace-loving nations to maintain the peace. Hope was not enough to beat back the aggressors as long as the peace-loving nations were unwilling to come to each other's defense. The aggressors were beaten back only when the peace-loving nations united to defend themselves.

If wars in the future are to be prevented the nations must be united in their determination to keep the peace under law.

Nothing is more essential to the future peace of the world than continued cooperation of the nations which had to muster the force necessary to defeat the conspiracy of the Axis powers to dominate the world.

While these great states have a special responsibility to enforce the peace, their responsibility is based upon the obligations resting upon all states, large and small, not to use force in international relations except in the defense of law. The responsibility of the great states is to serve and not to dominate the world.

To build a foundation of enduring peace we must not only work in harmony with our friends abroad, but we must have the united support of our own people. [. . .]

I appeal to every American, regardless of party, race, creed, or color, to support our efforts to build a strong and lasting United Nations Organization.

You, the Members of the Congress, surely know how I feel. Only with your help can I hope to complete one of the greatest tasks ever assigned to a public servant. With Divine guidance, and your help, we will find the new passage to a far better world, a kindly and friendly world, with just and lasting peace.

With confidence, I am depending upon all of you. To destroy greedy tyrants with dreams of world domination, we cannot continue in successive generations to sacrifice our finest youth. In the name of human decency and civilization, a more rational method of deciding national differences *must* and *will* be found!

America must assist suffering humanity back along the path of peaceful progress. This will require time and tolerance. We shall need also an abiding faith in the people, the kind of faith and courage which Franklin Delano Roosevelt always had!

Today, America has become one of the most powerful forces for good on earth. We must keep it so. We have achieved a world leadership which does not depend solely upon our military and naval might.

We have learned to fight with other nations in common defense of our freedom. We must now learn to live with other nations for our mutual good. We must learn to trade more with other nations so that there may be—for our mutual advantage—increased production, increased employment, and better standards of living throughout the world.

May we Americans all live up to our glorious heritage.

In that way, America may well lead the world to peace and prosperity.

At this moment, I have in my heart a prayer. As I have assumed my heavy duties, I humbly pray Almighty God, in the words of King Solomon: "Give therefore thy servant an understanding heart to judge thy people, that I may discern between good and bad; for who is able to judge this thy so great a people?"

I ask only to be a good and faithful servant of my Lord and my people.

★ The Atomic Bomb ★

The war in the Pacific continued through the summer of 1945. Truman, Stalin, and Clement Attlee, Churchill's successor, met at Potsdam, near Berlin in July. Agreeing on arrangements for a joint occupation of Germany, they also demanded that Japan surrender unconditionally. When Japan refused, President Truman, in perhaps the most agonizing decision of modern history, ordered an atomic bomb dropped on the industrial city of Hiroshima on August 6, 1945. Three days later, another bomb wiped out Nagasaki. Together, the two blasts killed about 200,000 people! On August 14, Truman announced that Japan had accepted the Potsdam terms. The most costly and terrifying war in history had ended, the hope for a better world now dawned. In this statement, Truman announced the first use of the atomic bomb.

Sixteen hours ago an American airplane dropped one bomb on Hiroshima and destroyed its usefulness to the enemy. That bomb had more power than 20,000 tons of TNT. It had more than two thousand times the blast power of the British "Grand Slam," which is the largest bomb ever yet used in the history of warfare.

The Japanese began the war from the air at Pearl Harbor. They have been repaid manyfold. And the end is not yet. With this bomb we have now added a new and revolutionary increase in destruction to supplement the growing power of our armed forces. In their present form these bombs are now in production and even more powerful forms are in development.

It is an atomic bomb. It is a harnessing of the basic power of the universe. The force from which the sun draws its power has been loosed against those who brought war to the Far East.

Before 1939, it was the accepted belief of scientists that it was theoretically possible to release atomic energy. But no one knew any practical method of doing it. By 1942, however, we knew that the Germans were working feverishly to find a way to add atomic energy to the other engines of war with which they hoped to enslave the world. But they failed. We may be grateful to Providence that the Germans got the V-1s and V-2s late and in limited quantities and even more grateful that they did not get the atomic bomb at all.

The battle of the laboratories held fateful risks for us as well as the battles of the air, land, and sea, and we have now won the battle of the laboratories as we have won the other battles. [. . .]

The United States had available the large number of scientists of distinction in the many needed areas of knowledge. It had the tremendous industrial and financial resources necessary for the project and they could be devoted to it without undue impairment of other vital war work. In the United States the laboratory work and the production plants, on which a substantial start had already been made, would be out of reach of enemy bombing, while at that time Britain was exposed to constant air attack and was still threatened with the possibility of invasion. For these reasons Prime Minister Churchill and President Roosevelt agreed that it was wise to carry on the project here. We now have two great plants and many lesser works devoted to the production of atomic power. Employment during peak construction numbered 125,000 and over 65,000 individuals are even now engaged in operating the plants. Many have worked there for two and a half years. Few know what they have been producing. [. . .] We have spent $2 billion on the greatest scientific gamble in history—and won.

But the greatest marvel is not the size of the enterprise, its secrecy, nor its cost, but the achievement of scientific brains in putting together infinitely complex pieces of knowledge held by many men in different fields of science into a workable plan. And hardly less marvelous has been the capacity of industry to design and of labor to operate, the machines and methods to do things never done before so that the brainchild of many minds came forth in physical shape and performed as it was supposed to do. Both science and industry worked under the direction of the United States Army, which achieved a unique success in managing so diverse a problem in the advancement of knowledge in an amazingly short time. It is doubtful if such another combination could be got together in the world. What has been done is the greatest achievement of organized science in history. It was done under pressure and without failure.

We are now prepared to obliterate more rapidly and completely every productive enterprise the Japanese have above ground in any city. We shall destroy their docks, their factories, and their communications. Let there be no mistake; we shall completely destroy Japan's power to make war.

It was to spare the Japanese people from utter destruction that the ultimatum of July 26 was issued at Potsdam. Their leaders promptly rejected that ultimatum. If they do not now accept our terms they may expect a rain of ruin from the air, the like of which has never been seen on this earth. Behind this air attack will follow sea and land forces in such number that and power as they have not yet seen and with the fighting skill of which they are already well aware.

The Secretary of War, who has kept in personal touch with all phases of the project, will immediately make public a statement giving further details.

His statement will give facts concerning the sites at Oak Ridge near Knoxville, Tennessee, and at Richland, near Pasco, Washington, and an installation near Santa Fe, New Mexico. Although the workers at the sites have been making materials to be used producing the greatest destructive force in history they have not themselves been in danger beyond that of many other occupations, for the utmost care has been taken of their safety.

The fact that we can release atomic energy ushers in a new era in man's understanding of nature's forces. Atomic energy may in the future supplement the power that now comes from coal, oil, and falling water, but at present it cannot be produced on a basis to compete with them commercially. Before that comes there must be a long period of intensive research. It has never been the habit of the scientists of this country or the policy of this government to withhold from the world scientific knowledge. Normally, therefore, everything about the work with atomic energy would be made public.

But under the present circumstances it is not intended to divulge the technical processes of production or all the military applications, pending further examination of possible methods of protecting us and the rest of the world from the danger of sudden destruction.

I shall recommend that the Congress of the United States consider promptly the establishment of an appropriate commission to control the production and use of atomic power within the United States. I shall give further consideration and make further recommendations to the Congress as to how atomic power can become a powerful and forceful influence towards the maintenance of world peace.

The Truman Doctrine

The Truman Doctrine of 1947 provided military and economic aid for Greece and Turkey. Both countries were in danger of falling to totalitarian governments and needed massive assistance to survive. Civil war had broken out in Greece. In Turkey, there was fear of an imminent Russian invasion. The British government, unable to maintain its longtime commitment to these countries, urged the United States to accept the responsibility of preserving democratic governments within these two nations.

President Truman concurred. He warned that if the United States did not give aid to Greece and Turkey to contain communism, then democratic governments everywhere would be threatened. "If we falter in our leadership, we may endanger the peace of the world—and we shall surely endanger the welfare of our own nation." Congress approved. This policy became known as the Truman Doctrine.

The gravity of the situation which confronts the world today necessitates my appearance before a joint session of the Congress. The foreign policy and the national security of this country are involved. One aspect of the present situation, which I wish to present to you at this time for your consideration and decision, concerns Greece and Turkey.

The United States has received from the Greek Government an urgent appeal for financial and economic assistance. Preliminary reports from the American Economic Mission now in Greece and reports from the American Ambassador in Greece corroborate the statement of the Greek Government that assistance is imperative if Greece is to survive as a free nation.

I do not believe that the American people and the Congress wish to turn a deaf ear to the appeal of the Greek Government.

Greece is not a rich country. Lack of sufficient natural resources has always forced the Greek people to work hard to make both ends meet. Since 1940, this industrious and peace loving country has suffered invasion, four years of cruel enemy occupation, and bitter internal strife.

When forces of liberation entered Greece they found that the retreating Germans had destroyed virtually all the railways, roads, port facilities, communications, and merchant marine. More than a thousand villages had been burned. Eighty-five per cent of the children were tubercular. Livestock, poultry, and draft animals had almost disappeared. Inflation had wiped out practically all savings.

As a result of these tragic conditions, a militant minority, exploiting human want and misery, was able to create political chaos which, until now, has made economic recovery impossible.

Greece is today without funds to finance the importation of those goods which are essential to bare subsistence. Under these circumstances the people of Greece cannot make progress in solving their problems of reconstruction. Greece is in desperate need of financial and economic assistance to enable it to resume purchases of food, clothing, fuel and seeds. These are indispensable for the subsistence of its people and are obtainable only from abroad. Greece must have help to import the goods necessary to restore internal order and security, so essential for economic and political recovery.

The Greek Government has also asked for the assistance of experienced American administrators, economists and technicians to insure that the financial and other aid given to Greece shall be used effectively in creating a stable and self-sustaining economy and in improving its public administration.

The very existence of the Greek state is today threatened by the terrorist activities of several thousand armed men, led by Communists, who defy the government's authority at a number of points, particularly along the northern boundaries. A Commission appointed by the United Nations Security Council is at present investigating disturbed conditions in northern Greece and alleged border violations along the frontier between Greece on the one hand and Albania, Bulgaria, and Yugoslavia on the other.

Meanwhile, the Greek Government is unable to cope with the situation. The Greek army is small and poorly equipped. It needs supplies and equipment if it is to restore the authority of the government throughout Greek territory. Greece must have assistance if it is to become a self-supporting and self-respecting democracy.

The United States must supply that assistance. We have already extended to Greece certain types of relief and economic aid but these are inadequate.

There is no other country to which democratic Greece can turn.

No other nation is willing and able to provide the necessary support for a democratic Greek government. [. . .]

We have considered how the United Nations might assist in this crisis. But the situation is an urgent one requiring immediate action and the United Nations and its related organizations are not in a position to extend help of the kind that is required.

It is important to note that the Greek Government has asked for our aid in utilizing effectively the financial and other assistance we may give to Greece, and in improving its public administration. It is of the utmost importance that we supervise the use of any funds made available to Greece; in such a manner that each dollar spent will count toward making Greece self-supporting, and will help to build an economy in which a healthy democracy can flourish.

No government is perfect. One of the chief virtues of a democracy, however, is that its defects are always visible and under democratic processes can be pointed out and corrected. The government of Greece is not perfect. Nevertheless it represents eighty-five per cent of the members of the Greek Parliament who were chosen in an election last year. Foreign observers, including 692 Americans, considered this election to be a fair expression of the views of the Greek people.

The Greek Government has been operating in an atmosphere of chaos and extremism. It has made mistakes. The extension of aid by this country does not mean that the United States condones everything that the Greek Government has done or will do. We have condemned in the past, and we condemn now, extremist measures of the right or the left. We have in the past advised tolerance, and we advise tolerance now.

Greece's neighbor, Turkey, also deserves our attention.

The future of Turkey as an independent and economically sound state is clearly no less important to the freedom-loving peoples of the world than the future of Greece. The circumstances in which Turkey finds itself today are considerably different from those of Greece. Turkey has been spared the disasters that have beset Greece. And during the war, the United States and Great Britain furnished Turkey with material aid.

Nevertheless, Turkey now needs our support.

Since the war Turkey has sought financial assistance from Great Britain and the United States for the purpose of effecting that modernization necessary for the maintenance of its national integrity. That integrity is essential to the preservation of order in the Middle East.

The British government has informed us that, owing to its own difficulties it can no longer extend financial or economic aid to Turkey. As in the case of Greece, if Turkey is to have the assistance it needs, the United States must supply it. We are the only country able to provide that help.

I am fully aware of the broad implications involved if the United States extends assistance to Greece and Turkey, and I shall discuss these implications with you at this time.

One of the primary objectives of the foreign policy of the United States is the creation of conditions in which we and other nations will be able to work out a way of life free from coercion. This was a fundamental issue in the war with Germany and Japan. Our victory was won over countries which sought to impose their will, and their way of life, upon other nations.

To ensure the peaceful development of nations, free from coercion, the United States has taken a leading part in establishing the United Nations, The United Nations is designed to make possible lasting freedom and independence for all its members. We shall not realize our objectives, however, unless we are willing to help free peoples to maintain their free institutions and their national integrity against aggressive movements that seek to impose upon them totalitarian regimes. This is no more than a frank recognition that totalitarian regimes imposed on free peoples, by direct or indirect aggression, undermine the foundations of international peace and hence the security of the United States.

The peoples of a number of countries of the world have recently had totalitarian regimes forced upon them against their will. The Government of the United States has made frequent protests against coercion and intimidation, in violation of the Yalta agreement, in Poland, Rumania, and Bulgaria. I must also state that in a number of other countries there have been similar developments.

Paper poster for Truman.

Truman attempted to continue the work of the New Deal in the domestic field. His instincts led him to sympathize with the liberal principles of his predecessor, but the mood of the country appeared to be increasingly conservative. In several messages to Congress, he proposed additional federal aid for housing and education, and a fair-employment practices law to prohibit discrimination based on race, religion, or national origin. But the President was often at odds with Congress, especially with southern Democrats and most Republicans who claimed these programs would create a welfare state.

At the present moment in world history nearly every nation must choose between alternative ways of life. The choice is too often not a free one.

One way of life is based upon the will of the majority, and is distinguished by free institutions, representative government, free elections, guarantees of individual liberty, freedom of speech and religion, and freedom from political oppression.

The second way of life is based upon the will of a minority forcibly imposed upon the majority. It relies upon terror and oppression, a controlled press and

Though Truman's aid programs were intended to help the nations of Europe rebuild after World War II, the United States itself had economic problems during Truman's presidency. The difficulties of transition from the controlled economy of war to the relatively free economy of peace were many. The chief domestic problems involved demobilization and shortages. In 1945, the supply of meat had reached a new low; razor blades, nylons, electrical appliances, automobiles, and cigarettes were virtually unobtainable. Inflation became alarming as Americans had earned money at unprecedented rates, and now tried to spend it as never before. Government figures showed a rise of 33 percent in living costs between 1941 and 1945. The postwar years witnessed widespread labor-management disputes as workers sought to preserve their wartime gains in earnings. Industry, on the other hand, pressed for relief from scores of federal controls. In 1946, 4.7 million workers went on strike, losing working time that amounted to 110.7 million man-days. Through all the conflicts of reconverting to a peacetime economy, Truman's political strength steadily declined. On November 5, 1946, the Republicans, making use of the slogan "Had enough?" won control of both houses of Congress for the first time since 1930.

radio; fixed elections, and the suppression of personal freedoms.

I believe that it must be the policy of the United States to support free peoples who are resisting attempted subjugation by armed minorities or by outside pressures.

I believe that we must assist free peoples to work out their own destinies in their own way.

I believe that our help should be primarily through economic and financial aid which is essential to economic stability and orderly political processes.

The world is not static, and the status quo is not sacred. But we cannot allow changes in the status quo in violation of the Charter of the United Nations by such methods as coercion, or by such subterfuges as political infiltration. In helping free and independent nations to maintain their freedom, the United States will be giving effect to the principles of the Charter of the United Nations.

It is necessary only to glance at a map to realize that the survival and integrity of the Greek nation are of grave importance in a much wider situation. If Greece should fall under the control of an armed minority, the effect upon its neighbor, Turkey, would be immediate and serious. Confusion and disorder might well spread throughout the entire Middle East.

Moreover, the disappearance of Greece as an independent state would have a profound effect upon those countries in Europe whose peoples are struggling against great difficulties to maintain their freedoms and their independence while they repair the damages of war.

It would be an unspeakable tragedy if these countries, which have struggled so long against overwhelming odds, should lose that victory for which they sacrificed so much. Collapse of free institutions and loss of independence would be disastrous not only for them but for the world. Discouragement and possibly failure would quickly be the lot of neighboring peoples striving to maintain their freedom and independence.

Should we fail to aid Greece and Turkey in this fateful hour, the effect will be far reaching to the West as well as to the East.

We must take immediate and resolute action.

I therefore ask the Congress to provide authority for assistance to Greece and Turkey in the amount of $400,000,000 for the period ending June 30, 1948. In requesting these funds, I have taken into consideration the maximum amount of relief assistance which would be furnished to Greece out of the $350,000,000 which I recently requested that the Congress authorize for the prevention of starvation and suffering in countries devastated by the war.

In addition to funds, I ask the Congress to authorize the detail of American civilian and military personnel to Greece and Turkey, at the request of those countries, to assist in the tasks of reconstruction, and for the purpose of supervising the use of such financial and material assistance as may be furnished. I recommend that authority also be provided for the instruction and training of selected Greek and Turkish personnel.

Finally, I ask that the Congress provide authority which will permit the speediest and most effective use, in terms of needed commodities, supplies, and equipment, of such funds as may be authorized.

If further funds, or further authority, should be needed for purposes indicated in this message, I shall not hesitate to bring the situation before the Congress. On this subject the Executive and Legislative branches of the Government must work together.

This is a serious course upon which we embark.

I would not recommend it except that the alternative is much more serious. The United States contributed $341,000,000,000 toward winning World War II. This is an investment in world freedom and world peace.

The assistance that I am recommending for Greece and Turkey amounts to little more than 1 tenth of 1 per cent of this investment. It is only common sense that we should safeguard this investment and make sure that it was not in vain.

The seeds of totalitarian regimes are nurtured by misery and want. They spread and grow in the evil soil of poverty and strife. They reach their full growth when the hope of a people for a better life has died. We must keep that hope alive.

The free peoples of the world look to us for support in maintaining their freedoms.

If we falter in our leadership, we may endanger the peace of the world— and we shall surely endanger the welfare of our own nation.

Great responsibilities have been placed upon us by the swift movement of events.

I am confident that the Congress will face these responsibilities squarely.

The Marshall Plan

The situation in Europe was desperate in 1947. There were short-ages of food, fuel, and raw materials. Money to rebuild industries was needed immediately. Indeed, the Continent lay in shambles, making it an ideal breeding ground for totalitarianism. Realizing that a similar situation had encouraged the rise of dictators after World War I, the Truman administration took the lead in establishing an aid program to encourage Europe's economic reconstruction. American leaders also feared that Europe's faltering economy might trigger a recession at home. In June 1947, Secretary of State George C. Marshall proposed that the United States finance a massive recovery program to restore the European economies. Although the Marshall Plan was offered to all European nations, the Soviet Union and its satellites refused to participate. The Marshall Plan proved to be an enormous success. During the Truman years, the United States provided more than $12 billion in economic aid to sixteen countries in Western Europe over a four-year period. In retrospect, the Marshall Plan both stabilized Western Europe and heightened the Cold War as a clear east-west division emerged. Secretary Marshall outlined his plan in a speech at Harvard University.

I need not tell you gentlemen that the world situation is very serious. That must be apparent to all intelligent people. I think one difficulty is that the problem is one of such enormous complexity that the very mass of facts presented to the public by press and radio make it exceedingly difficult for the man in the street to reach a clear appraisement of the situation. Furthermore, the people of this country are distant from the troubled areas of the earth and it is hard for them to comprehend the plight and consequent reaction of the long-suffering peoples, and the effect of those reactions on their governments in connection with our efforts to promote peace in the world.

In considering the requirements for the rehabilitation of Europe the physical loss of life, the visible destruction of cities, factories, mines, and railroads was correctly estimated, but it has become obvious during recent months that this visible destruction was probably less serious than the dislocation of the entire fabric of European economy. For the past 10 years conditions have been highly abnormal. The feverish maintenance of the war effort engulfed all aspects of national economics. Machinery has fallen into disrepair or is entirely obsolete. Under the arbitrary and destructive Nazi rule, virtually every possible enterprise was geared into the German war machine. Long-standing commercial ties, private institutions, banks, insurance companies and shipping companies disappeared, through the loss of capital, absorption through nationalization or by simple destruction. In many countries, confidence in the local currency has been severely shaken. The breakdown of the business structure of Europe during the war was complete. Recovery has been seriously retarded by the fact that two years after the close of hostilities a peace settlement with Germany and Austria has not been agreed upon. But even given a more prompt solution of these difficult problems, the rehabilitation of the economic structure of Europe quite evidently will require a much longer time and greater effort than had been foreseen.

There is a phase of this matter which is both interesting and serious. The farmer has always produced the foodstuffs to exchange with the city dweller for the other necessities of life. This division of labor is the basis of modern civilization. At the present time it is threatened with breakdown. The town and city industries are not producing adequate goods to exchange with the food-producing farmer. Raw materials and fuel are in short supply. Machinery is lacking or worn out. The farmer or the peasant cannot find the goods for sale which he desires to purchase. So the sale of his farm produce for money which he cannot use seems to him unprofitable transaction. He, therefore, has withdrawn many fields from crop cultivation and is using them for grazing. He feeds more grain to stock and finds for himself and his family an ample supply of food, however short he may be on clothing and the other ordinary gadgets of civilization. Meanwhile people in the cities are short of food and fuel. So the governments are forced to use their foreign money and credits to procure these necessities abroad. This process exhausts funds which are urgently needed for reconstruction. Thus a very serious situation is rapidly developing which bodes no good for the world. The modern system of the division of labor upon which the exchange of products is based is in danger of breaking down.

The truth of the matter is that Europe's requirements for the next three or four years of foreign food and other essential products—principally from America—are so much greater than her present ability to pay that she must have substantial additional help, or face economic, social, and political deterioration of a very grave character.

The remedy lies in breaking the vicious circle and restoring the confidence of the European people in the economic future of their own countries and of Europe as a whole. The manufacturer and the farmer throughout wide areas must be able and willing to exchange their products for currencies the continuing value of which is not open to question.

Campaign pin showing support for Truman's agenda. As president, Truman advocated an expansion of Roosevelt's depression-born policies in a period of unprecedented prosperity.

Aside from the demoralizing effect on the world at large and the possibilities of disturbances arising as a result of the desperation of the people concerned, the consequences to the economy of the United States should be apparent to all. It is logical that the United States should do whatever it is able to do to assist in the return of normal economic health in the world, without which there can be no political stability and no assured peace. Our policy is directed not against any country or doctrine but against hunger, poverty, desperation, and chaos. Its purpose should be the revival of working economy in the world so as to permit the emergence of political and social conditions in which free institutions can exist. Such assistance, I am convinced, must not be on a piecemeal basis as various crises develop. Any assistance that this Government may render in the future should provide a cure rather than a mere palliative. Any government that is willing to assist in the task of recovery will find full cooperation, I am sure, on the part of the United States Government. Any government which maneuvers to block the recovery of other countries cannot expect help from us. Furthermore, governments, political parties, or groups which seek to perpetuate human misery in order to profit therefrom politically or otherwise will encounter the opposition of the United States.

The 1948 election is especially interesting because almost every political commentator and public opinion analyst agreed that President Harry Truman had little chance for election. Between the middle of 1946 and October 1947, food costs rose 40 percent and clothing 19 percent. Truman proposed a return to wartime wage and price ceilings. Congress passed a much milder bill in December 1947. However, the sharpest conflict between the President and Congress occurred over labor legislation. Influenced by the mass work stoppages, the Republican dominated Eightieth Congress passed a strong labor bill over the President's veto called the National Labor Relations Act of 1947, or Taft-Hartley Act. Labor organizations bitterly denounced the bill, which among other things banned secondary boycotts, established new rules for collective bargaining, and required unions to file complete financial statements with the Department of Labor. The Taft-Hartley law promised to be one of the major issues in the 1948 election, as unions labeled it the "slave labor act" and pledged to defeat all who had voted for it.

It is already evident that, before the United States Government can proceed much further in its efforts to alleviate the situation and help start the European world on its way to recovery, there must be some agreement among the countries of Europe as to the requirements of the situation and the part those countries themselves will take in order to give proper effect to whatever action might be undertaken by this Government. It would be neither fitting nor efficacious for this Government to undertake to draw up unilaterally a program designed to place Europe on its feet economically. This is the business of the Europeans. The initiative, I think, must come from Europe. The role of this country should consist of friendly aid in the drafting of a European program so far as it may be practical for us to do so. The program should be a joint one, agreed to by a number, if not all European nations.

An essential part of any successful action on the part of the United States is an understanding on the part of the people of America of the character of the problem and the remedies to be applied. Political passion and prejudice should have no part. With foresight, and a willingness on the part of our people to face up to the vast responsibilities which history has clearly placed upon our country, the difficulties I have outlined can and will be overcome.

Wallace Announces His Candidacy

To add to the woe of the Democrats, two other groups entered the 1948 presidential race, each threatening to cut into Truman's vote. In a radio speech on December 29, 1947, Henry A. Wallace, vice president during Roosevelt's third term, announced his decision to seek the presidency of a new party and outlined the main themes of his campaign. Wallace's Progressive Party was pledged to improve relations with the Soviet Union. It appeared that Wallace would receive many votes that usually went to the Democrats. In addition, some southern delegates bolted the Democratic convention over the civil rights plank; they formed the States' Rights Party and nominated Governor J. Strom Thurmond of South Carolina for the presidency.

On July 23, 1948, more than 3,000 delegates to the Progressive Party convention nominated Henry Wallace by acclamation. The newly formed party called for "an understanding between the Soviet Union and the United States"; removal from power of "the war-producing elite"; a repudiation of the Marshall Plan; the destruction of all atomic bombs; better housing; lower food prices; and an immediate end to segregation. The Wallace "movement" was labeled as being communist dominated and it was already in decline before the convention met.

For the past fifteen months I have traveled up and down, and back and forth across this country. I have talked with half a million people in public meetings and with thousands in private gatherings. I have been working for, and I shall continue to work for, peace and security.

Everywhere in the United States today, among farmers, workers, small business men and professional men and women, I find confusion, uncertainty and fear. The people don't ask, "Will there be another war?"—but "When will the war come?"

Everywhere I find that people are spending so much for food and rent that they cannot afford their customary services from the doctor and dentist. They don't ask, "Will there be another depression?" but "When will the real depression start?"

Peace and abundance mean so much to me that I have said at a dozen press conferences and in many speeches when asked about a third party, "If the Democratic Party continues to be a party of war and depression, I will see to it that the people have a chance to vote for prosperity and peace."

To those who have come to me asking the conditions of my adherence to the present Democratic Administration, I have said, "Let the Administration repudiate universal military training and rid itself of the Wall Street-military team that is leading us toward war."

I have insisted that the Democratic Administration curb the ever-growing power and profits of monopoly and take concrete steps to preserve the living standards of the American people. I have demanded that the Democratic Administration cease its attacks on the civil liberties of Americans. In speeches in the North and in the South at non-segregated meetings I have stated the simple truth that segregation and discrimination of any kind or character have no place in America.

My terms to the Democratic high command have been well known.

By their actions and finally by their words, they have said: "Henry

Wallace, we welcome your support but we will not change our policies."

In answering me, the Democratic leadership also gave its answer to millions of Americans who demand the right to vote for peace and prosperity. Thus, the leadership of the Democratic Party would deprive the American people of their rightful opportunity to choose between progress and reaction in 1948.

So far as the Republican Party is concerned, there is no hope—as George Norris, Fiorello LaGuardia, and Wendell Willkie long ago found out.

When the old parties rot, the people have a right to be heard through a new party. They asserted that right when the Democratic Party was founded under Jefferson in the struggle against the Federalist Party of war and privilege of his time. They won it again when the Republican Party was organized in Lincoln's day. The people must again have an opportunity to speak out with their votes in 1948.

The lukewarm liberals sitting on two chairs say, "Why throw away your vote?" I say a vote for the new party in 1948 will be the most valuable vote you have ever cast or ever will cast.

The bigger the peace vote in 1948, the more definitely the world will know that the United States is not behind the bipartisan reactionary war policy which is dividing the world into two armed camps and making inevitable the day when American soldiers will be lying in their Arctic suits in the Russian snow.

There is no real fight between a Truman and a Republican. Both stand for a policy which opens the door to war in our lifetime and makes war certain for our children.

Stop saying, "I don't like it but I am going to vote for the lesser of two evils." Rather than accept either evil, come out boldly, stand upright as men and women and say so loudly all the world can hear—

"We are voting peace and security for ourselves and our children's children. We are fighting for old-fashioned Americanism at the polls in 1948. We are fighting for freedom of speech and freedom of assembly. We are fighting to end racial discrimination. We are fighting for lower prices. We are fighting for

Large celluloid button with Franklin D. Roosevelt's shadow shown behind Wallace.

free labor unions, for jobs, and for homes in which we can decently live."

We have just passed through the holiday season when every radio and every church proclaimed the joyous tidings of peace. Every year at this time the hearts of the American people swell with genuine good will toward all mankind. We are a kindly, well-meaning people.

But the holiday season soon passes and one of the first items on the agenda of the new Congress is universal military training. I say the first political objective of progressives is the defeat of this bill which would deliver our 18-year-olds over to the Army and cost the nation $2 billion a year.

Universal military training is the first decisive step on the road toward fascism. We shall fight it to the limit and all Congressmen who vote for it.

The American people read that they are paying fantastic appropriations for military adventures in Greece, Turkey, China—and billions for armaments here at home. Slowly it dawns on us that these newspaper headlines have stepped into our every-day lives at the grocery store when we pay $1 for butter, 95 cents for eggs, and 90 cents for meat.

We suddenly realize that you can't have all the people of the world getting ready for the next war without paying for it in their daily lives with less food, clothing, and housing. War preparations create record profits for big business but only false prosperity for the people—their purchasing power shrinks as prices rise, their needs go unfilled, and they are burdened with new debts.

Yes, corporation profits are over three times what they were in 1939, but every family is paying for our war policy at the grocery store.

A new party must stand for a positive peace program of abundance and security, not scarcity and war. We can prevent depression and war if we only organize for peace in the same comprehensive way we organize for war.

I personally was for the humanitarian aspects of the Marshall plan long before it was announced. Because I saw the post-war need of helping human beings, I was accused of wanting a quart of milk for every Hottentot.

I pushed for help for Greece against the opposition of the Administration eight months before the Truman doctrine was announced. But I have fought and shall continue to fight programs which give guns to people when they want plows.

I fight the Truman doctrine and the Marshall plan as applied because they divide Europe into two warring camps. Those whom we buy politically with our food will soon desert us. They will pay us in the base coin of temporary gratitude and then turn to hate us because our policies are destroying their freedom.

We are restoring western Europe and Germany through United States agencies rather than United Nations agencies because we want to hem Russia in. We are acting in the same way as France and England after the last war and the end result will be the same—confusion, depression, and war.

It just doesn't need to happen. The cost of organizing for peace, prosperity, and progress is infinitely less than organizing for war.

We who believe this will be called "Russian tools" and "Communists." Let the fear mongers not distort and becloud the issues by name calling. We are not for Russia and we are not for communism, but we recognize Hitlerite methods when we see them in our own land and we denounce the men who engage in such name calling as enemies of the human race who would rather have World War III than put forth a genuine effort to bring about a peaceful settlement of differences.

One thing I want to make clear to both Russia and the United States— peace requires real understanding between our peoples. Russia has as much to gain from peace as the United States, and just as we here fight against the spreaders of hate and falsehood against Russia, the Russian leaders can make a great contribution by restraining those extremists who try to widen the gap between our two great countries.

I insist that the United States be fully secure until there is a real peace between this country and Russia and until there is an international police force stronger than the military establishment of any nation, including Russia and the United States.

I am utterly against any kind of imperialism or expansionism, whether sponsored by Britain, Russia, or the United States, and I call on Russia as well as the United States to look at all our differences objectively and free from that prejudice which the hate mongers have engendered on both sides.

What the world needs is a United Nations disarmament conference to rid humanity for all time of the threat not only of atomic bombs but also of all other methods of mass destruction. [. . .]

I announce tonight that I shall run as an independent candidate for President of the United States in 1948.

Thousands of people all over the United States have asked me to engage in this great fight. The people are on the march. I hope that you who are listening to me tonight will lead the forces of peace, progress, and prosperity in your communities and throughout our country. Will you let me know that you have come out fighting against the powers of evil?

We have assembled a Gideon's army—small in number, powerful in conviction, ready for action. We have said with Gideon, "Let those who are fearful and trembling depart." For every fearful one who leaves there will be a thousand to take his place. A just cause is worth a hundred armies.

We face the future unfettered by any principle but the principle of general welfare. We owe no allegiance to any group which does not serve that welfare. By God's grace, the people's peace will usher in the century of the common man.

Dewey Accepts the Nomination

The Republican Convention opened in Philadelphia on June 21, 1948. A feeling of victory was in the air. The Gallup Poll showed Truman's approval rating at 36 percent, down from 60 percent a year before. Congresswoman Clare Boothe Luce told the cheering delegates that Truman was a "gone goose." Thomas E. Dewey, the governor of New York who had opposed Roosevelt in the 1944 election, was nominated on the third ballot. This was the first time in the party's history that a defeated candidate had been renominated. Dewey chose Earl Warren, governor of California, for his running mate. *Time* and *Newsweek* agreed that only a miracle could save Truman from an overwhelming defeat by two youthful, progressive governors from two crucial states that were needed for victory. Thomas Dewey accepted the Republican Party nomination with this speech.

You, the elected representatives of our Republican Party have again given to me the highest honor you can bestow—your nomination for President of the United States.

I thank you with all my heart for your friendship and confidence. I am profoundly sensible of the responsibility that goes with it. I pray God that I may deserve this opportunity to serve our country. I come to you unfettered by a single obligation or promise to any living person, free to join with you in selecting to serve our nation the finest men and women in the nation, free to unite our party and our country in meeting the grave challenge of our time.

United we can match this challenge with depth of understanding and largeness of spirit; with a unity which is above recrimination, above partisanship, above self-interest. These are articles of faith from which the greatness of America has been fashioned. Our people are eager to know again the upsurging [sic] power of that faith. They are turning to us to put such a faith at the heart of our national life. That is what we are called to do. That is what we will do.

In this historic convention you have had placed in nomination before you six other candidates, all high-minded men of character and ability and deeply devoted to their country—Senator Raymond E. Baldwin, General Douglas MacArthur, Governor Harold E. Stassen, Senator Robert A. Taft, Senator Arthur Vandenberg, and Governor Earl Warren. It has been a difficult choice in an honorable contest. It has been a stirring demonstration of the life and vitality and ideals of our Republican Party.

There has been honest contention, spirited disagreement, hot argument. But let no one be misled. You are given a moving and dramatic proof of how *Americans*, who honestly differ, close ranks and move forward, for the nation's well being, shoulder to shoulder.

The responsibility and the opportunity that have come to our party are the greatest in the history of free government. For tonight our future—our peace, our prosperity, the very fate of freedom—hangs in a precarious balance.

Mere victory in an election is not our task or our purpose. Our task is to fill our victory with such meaning that mankind everywhere, yearning for freedom, will take heart and move forward out of this desperate darkness into the light of freedom's promise.

Our platform proclaims the guideposts that will mark our steadfast and certain endeavor in a fearful world. This magnificent statement of principles is concise and to the point.

You unanimously adopted it. I proudly support it. It will be the heart of the message I will take to the country. After January 20th, it will be the *cornerstone* of our Republican administration.

We are a united party. Our nation stands tragically in need of that same unity.

Our people are turning away from the meaner things that divide us. They yearn to move to higher ground, to find a common purpose in the finer things which unite us. We must be the instrument of that aspiration. We must be the means by which America's full powers are released and this uncertain future filled again, with opportunity. That is our pledge. That will be the fruit of our victory.

If this unity is to be won and kept, it must have great dimensions. Its boundaries must be far above and beyond politics. Freedom can be saved—it can only be saved—if free men everywhere make this unity their common cause.

Celluloid button for Dewey and Warren.

Unity in such a cause *must* be the chief cornerstone of peace. A peace won at the expense of liberty is a peace too dearly bought. Such a peace would not endure. Above all other purposes, we must labor by every peaceful means to build a world order founded upon justice and righteousness. That kind of world will have peace. That kind of peace *will* be worth having. That is the crowning responsibility that our people have laid upon us. That is the crowning task to which we dedicate ourselves.

The unity we seek is more than material. It is more than a matter of things and measures. It is most of all spiritual.

Our problem is not *outside ourselves*. Our problem is within ourselves. We have found the means to blow our world, physically, apart. We have yet to find the means to put together the world's broken pieces, to bind up its wounds, to make a good society, a community of men of good will that fits our dreams. We have devised noble plans for a new world. Without a new spirit, our noblest plans will come to nothing.

Painted metal figure of Dewey.

We pray that, in the days ahead, a full measure of that spirit may be ours.

The next Presidential term will see the completion of the first half of the twentieth century. So far it has been a century of amazing progress and of terrible tragedy. We have seen the world transformed. We have seen mankind's age long struggle against nature crowned by extraordinary success.

Yet our triumphs have been darkened by bitter defeats in the equally ancient struggle of men to live together in peace, security and understanding.

This age of progress, this twentieth century, has been dominated by two terrible world wars and, between the wars, the worst economic depression in the history of mankind.

We must learn to do better. The period that is drawing to a close has been one of scientific achievement. The era that is opening before us must be

WIN WITH DEWEY AND WARREN

Tin automobile license attachment promoting the Republican candidates.

In 1953, President Dwight Eisenhower nominated Earl Warren to be the 14th Chief Justice of the Supreme Court, a position he held until his retirement sixteen years later. He presided over the Court during a period of sweeping changes in U. S. constitutional law especially in the areas of race relations and criminal procedure. On November 29, 1963, President Lyndon Johnson appointed Warren chairman of a commission to investigate the assassination of President John Kennedy. The report of the Warren Commission was submitted one year later.

a period of human and spiritual achievement.

We propose to continue to carry forward the great technological gains of our age. We shall harness the unimaginable possibilities of atomic energy, to bring men and women a larger, fuller life. But there is something more important than all this. With all the energy, intelligence and determination which mortal heart and mind can bring to the task, we must solve the problem of establishing a just and lasting peace in the world, and of securing to our own and other like-minded people the blessing of freedom and opportunity.

To me, to be a Republican in this hour is to dedicate one's life to the freedom of men. As long as the world is half free and half slave, we must peacefully labor to help men everywhere to achieve liberty.

We have declared our goal to be a strong and free America in a free world of free men—free to speak their own minds, to develop new ideas, to publish what they believe, free to move from place to place, to choose occupations, to enjoy the fruits of their labor, free to worship God, each according to his own concept of His Grace and His Mercy.

When *these* rights are secure in the world, the permanent ideals of the Republican Party shall have been realized.

The ideals of the American people *are* the ideals of the Republican Party. We have lighted a *beacon* here in Philadelphia in this cradle of our own independence. We have lighted a beacon to give eternal hope that men may live in liberty with human dignity and before God and loving Him, stand erect and free.

Truman Accepts the Nomination

Truman's chances for election seemed slim as the Democratic Convention began its sessions in Philadelphia on July 12, 1948. Many delegates stayed at home and, on opening day, the galleries were largely empty. "You could cut the gloom with a corn knife," recalled Senator Alben W. Barkley. "The very air smelled of defeat." On July 14, the day scheduled for Truman's nomination and acceptance speech, the convention became involved in a bitter debate over the civil rights plank in the platform. Finally, at nearly midnight, Truman received the presidential nomination and 71-year-old Alben Barkley was chosen for vice president. Truman delivered his acceptance speech at 2 A.M. Speaking without notes, he emphatically declared: "Senator Barkley and I will win this election and make these Republicans like it—don't you forget that." Then the President announced that he was calling the Republican dominated Congress into special session with the challenge they enact the social and economic planks of their platform into law. The *New York Times* said that he had "set the convention on fire."

I am sorry that the microphones are in the way, but I must leave them the way they are because I have got to be able to see what I am doing—as I am always able to see what I am doing.

I can't tell you how very much I appreciate the honor which you have just conferred upon me. I shall continue to try to deserve it.

I accept the nomination.

And I want to thank this convention for its unanimous nomination of my good friend and colleague, Senator Barkley of Kentucky. He is a great man, and a great public servant. Senator Barkley and I will win this election and make these Republicans like it—don't you forget that!

We will do that because they are wrong and we are right, and I will prove it to you in just a few minutes.

This convention met to express the will and reaffirm the beliefs of the Democratic Party. There have been differences of opinion, and that is the democratic way. Those differences have been settled by a majority vote, as they should be.

Now it is time for us to get together and beat the common enemy. And that is up to you.

We have been working together for victory in a great cause. Victory has become a habit in our party. It has been elected four times in succession, and I am convinced it will be elected a fifth time in November.

The reason is that the people know that the Democratic Party is the people's party, and the Republican Party is the party of special interest, and it always has been and always will be.

The record of the Democratic Party is written in the accomplishments of the last 16 years. I don't need to repeat them. They have been very ably placed before this convention by the keynote speaker, the candidate for Vice President, and by the permanent chairman.

Confidence and security have been brought to the people by the

Democratic Party. Farm income has increased from less than $2.5 billion in 1932 to more than $18 billion in 1947. Never in the world were the farmers of any republic or any kingdom or any other country as prosperous as the farmers of the United States; and if they don't do their duty by the Democratic Party, they are the most ungrateful people in the world!

Wages and salaries in this country have increased from $29 billion in 1933 to more than $128 billion in 1947. That's labor, and labor never had but one friend in politics, and that is the Democratic Party and Franklin D. Roosevelt.

And I say to labor what I have said to the farmers: they are the most ungrateful people in the world if they pass the Democratic Party by this year.

The total national income has increased from less than $40 billion in 1933 to $203 billion in 1947, the greatest in all the history of the world. These benefits have been spread to all the people, because it is the business of the Democratic Party to see that the people get a fair share of these things.

This last, worst Eightieth Congress proved just the opposite for the Republicans.

The record on foreign policy of the Democratic Party is that the United States has been turned away permanently from isolationism, and we have converted the greatest and best of the Republicans to our viewpoint on that subject.

The United States has to accept its full responsibility for leadership in international affairs. We have been the backers and the people who organized and started the United Nations, first started under that great Democratic President, Woodrow Wilson, as the League of Nations. The League was sabotaged by the Republicans in 1920. And we must see that the United Nations continues a strong and growing body, so we can have everlasting peace in the world.

We removed trade barriers in the world, which is the best asset we can have for peace. Those trade barriers must not be put back into operation again.

We have started the foreign aid program, which means the recovery of Europe and China, and the Far East. We instituted the program for Greece and Turkey, and I will say to you that all these things were done in a cooperative and bipartisan manner. The Foreign Relations Committees of the Senate and House were taken into the full confidence of the President in every one of these moves, and don't let anybody tell you anything else.

As I have said time and time again, foreign policy should be the policy of the whole Nation and not the policy of one party or the other. Partisanship should stop at the water's edge; and I shall continue to preach that through this whole campaign.

I would like to say a word or two now on what I think the Republican philosophy is; and I will speak from actions and from history and from experience.

The situation in 1932 was due to the policies of the Republican Party control of the Government of the United States. The Republican Party, as I said a while ago, favors the privileged few and not the common everyday man. Ever since its inception, that party has been under the control of special privilege; and they have completely proved it in the Eightieth Congress. They proved it by the things they did to the people, and not for them. They proved it by the things they failed to do.

Now, let's look at some of them—just a few.

Time and time again I recommended extension of price control before it expired June 30, 1946. I asked for that extension in September 1945, in November 1945, in a Message on the State of the Union in 1946; and that price control legislation did not come to my desk until June 30, 1946, on the day on which it was supposed to expire. And it was such a rotten bill that I couldn't sign it. And 30 days after that, they sent me one just as bad. I had to sign it, because they quit and went home.

They said, when OPA died, that prices would adjust themselves for the benefit of the country. They have been adjusting themselves all right! They have gone all the way off the chart in adjusting themselves, at the expense of the consumer and for the benefit of the people that hold the goods.

I called a special session of the Congress in November 1947—November 17, 1947—and I set out a 10-point program for the welfare and benefit of this country, among other things standby controls. I got nothing. Congress has still done nothing.

Way back four-and-a-half years ago, while I was in the Senate, we passed a housing bill in the Senate known as the Wagner-Ellender-Taft bill. It was a bill to clear the slums in the big cities and to help to erect low-rent housing. That bill, as I said, passed the Senate four years ago. It died in the House. That bill was reintroduced in the Eightieth Congress as the Taft-Ellender-Wagner bill. The name was slightly changed, but it is practically the same bill. And it passed the Senate, but it was allowed to die in the House of Representatives; and they sat on that bill, and finally forced it out of the Banking and Currency Committee, and the Rules Committee took charge, and it still is in the Rules Committee.

But desperate pleas from Philadelphia in that convention that met here three weeks ago couldn't get that housing bill passed. They passed a bill they called a housing bill, which isn't worth the paper it's written on.

In the field of labor we needed moderate legislation to promote labor-management harmony, but Congress passed instead that so-called Taft-Hartley Act, which has disrupted labor-management relations and will cause strife and bitterness for years to come if it is not repealed, as the Democratic platform says it ought to be repealed.

On the Labor Department, the Republican platform of 1944 said, if they were in power, that they would build up a strong Labor Department. They have simply torn it up. Only one bureau is left that is functioning, and they cut the appropriation of that so it can hardly function.

I recommended an increase in the minimum wage. What did I get? Nothing. Absolutely nothing.

Poster for Truman and Barkley.

Old line New Deal liberals, led by Minneapolis Mayor Hubert Humphrey, had formed Americans for Democratic Action (ADA), a non-communist response to the Wallace movement. They backed Dwight Eisenhower, now president of Columbia University, who had become the favorite candidate of many Democrats as well as Republicans. When Eisenhower made it unmistakably clear that he would not run, the ADA announced its support for Supreme Court Justice William O. Douglas. Truman and his pledged delegates prevailed. But, Humphrey and his supporters fought for a civil rights plank in the platform promising a federal anti-lynching law, a federal anti-poll tax law, legislation guaranteeing fair employment regardless of race, and an end to segregation in the armed forces.

I suggested that the schools in this country are crowded, teachers underpaid, and that there is a shortage of teachers. One of our greatest national needs is more and better schools. I urged Congress to provide $300 million to aid the States in the present educational crisis. Congress did nothing about it. Time and again I have recommended improvements in the social security law, including extending protection to those not now covered, and increasing the amount of benefits, to reduce the eligibility age of women from 65 to 60 years.

Poster for Truman and Barkley with Missouri state Democratic candidates.

Several presidential candidates have had to cope with splits within their parties, but Truman faced a situation unprecedented in political history. He waged an aggressive campaign, relentlessly attacking the record of the Republican Party and reaffirming the principles of the New Deal. He defied the Dixiecrats and held on to the African-American vote in northern cities. He countered Wallace's attack with an aggressive defense of his foreign policy. Dewey, on the other hand, never caught the imagination of the voters. Truman, aware of the fight he had to make, campaigned across the country denouncing "the do-nothing, good-for-nothing Eightieth Congress."

Congress studied the matter for two years, but couldn't find time to extend or increase the benefits. But they did find the time to take social security benefits away from 750,000 people, and they passed that over my veto.

I have repeatedly asked the Congress to pass a health program. The nation suffers from lack of medical care. That situation can be remedied any time the Congress wants to act upon it.

Everybody knows that I recommended to the Congress the civil rights program. I did that because I believed it to be my duty under the Constitution. Some of the members of my own party disagree with me violently on this matter. But they stand up and do it openly! People can tell where they stand. But the Republicans all professed to be for these measures. But Congress failed to act. They had enough men to do it, they could have had cloture, they didn't have to have a filibuster. They had enough people in that Congress that would vote for cloture.

Now everybody likes to have low taxes, but we must reduce the national debt in times of prosperity. And when tax relief can be given, it ought to go to those who need it most and not those who need it least, as this Republican rich man's tax bill did when they passed it over my veto on the third try.

The first one of these was so rotten that they couldn't even stomach it themselves. They finally did send one that was somewhat improved, but it still helps the rich and sticks a knife into the back of the poor.

Now the Republicans came here a few weeks ago, and they wrote a platform. I hope you have all read that platform. They adopted the platform, and that platform had a lot of promises and statement of what the Republican Party is for, and what they would do if they were in power. They promised to do in that platform a lot of things I have been asking them to do that they have refused to do when they had the power.

The Republican platform cries about cruelly high prices. I have been trying to get them to do something about high prices ever since they met the first time.

Now listen! This is equally bad, and as cynical. The Republican platform comes out for slum clearance and low-rental housing. I have been trying to get them to pass that housing bill ever since they met the first time, and it is still resting in the Rules Committee, that bill.

The Republican platform favors educational opportunity and promotion of education. I have been trying to get Congress to do something about that ever since they came there, and that bill is at rest in the House of Representatives.

The Republican platform is for extending and increasing social security benefits. Think of that! Increasing social security benefits! Yet when they had the opportunity, they took 750,000 off the social security rolls!

I wonder if they think they can fool the people of the United States with such poppycock as that!

There is a long list of these promises in that Republican platform. If it weren't so late, I would tell you all about them. I have discussed a number of these failures of the Republican Eightieth Congress. Every one of them is important. Two of them are of major concern to nearly every American family. They failed to do anything about high prices; they failed to do anything about housing.

My duty as President requires that I use every means within my power to get the laws the people need on matters of such importance and urgency.

I am therefore calling this Congress back into session July 26th.

On the 26th day of July, which out in Missouri we call "Turnip Day," I am going to call Congress back and ask them to pass laws to halt rising prices, to meet the housing crisis—which they are saying they are for in their platform.

At the same time I shall ask them to act upon other vitally needed measures such as aid to education, which they say they are for; a national health program; civil rights legislation, which they say they are for; an increase in the minimum wage, which I doubt very much they are for; extension of social security coverage and increased benefits, which they say they are for; funds for projects needed in our program to provide public power and cheap electricity. By indirection, this Eightieth Congress has tried to sabotage the power policies the United States has pursued for 14 years. That power lobby is as bad as the real estate lobby, which is sitting on the housing bill.

I shall ask for adequate and decent laws for displaced persons in place of this anti-Semitic, anti-Catholic law which this Eightieth Congress passed.

Now, my friends, if there is any reality behind that Republican platform, we ought to get some action from a short session of the Eightieth Congress. They can do this job in 15 days, if they want to do it. They will still have time to go out and run for office.

They are going to try to dodge their responsibility. They are going to drag all the red herrings they can across this campaign, but I am here to say that Senator Barkley and I are not going to let them get away with it.

Now, what that worst Eightieth Congress does in this special session will be the test. The American people will not decide by listening to mere words, or by reading a mere platform. They will decide on the record, the record as it has been written. And in the record is the stark truth, that the battle lines of 1948 are the same as they were in 1932, when the Nation lay prostrate and helpless as a result of Republican misrule and inaction.

In 1932 we were attacking the citadel of special privilege and greed. We were fighting to drive the money changers from the temple. Today, in 1948, we are now the defenders of the stronghold of democracy and of equal opportunity, the haven of the ordinary people of this land and not of the favored classes or the powerful few. The battle cry is just the same now as it was in 1932, and I paraphrase the words of Franklin D. Roosevelt as he issued the challenge, in accepting nomination in Chicago: "This is more than a political call to arms. Give me your help, not to win votes alone, but to win in this new crusade to keep America secure and safe for its own people."

Now my friends, with the help of God and the wholehearted push which you can put behind this campaign, we can save this country from a continuation of the Eightieth Congress, and from misrule from now on.

I must have your help. You must get in and push, and win this election. The country can't afford another Republican Congress.

Platform of the States' Rights Party

On July 17, 1948, three days after Truman's nomination, some 300 conservative southern Democrats assembled in Birmingham, Alabama, for a convention of States' Rights Democrats (Dixiecrats). They named Governor J. Strom Thurmond of South Carolina for president. They denounced the civil rights planks of the Democratic platform and affirmed their belief in "the segregation of the races." If Thurmond and his running mate, Governor Fielding Wright of Mississippi could obtain all of the South's electoral votes, they might deny both Truman and Dewey an electoral majority. This would put the election into the House of Representatives, placing the South in a strong position. Thurmond was asked why he was breaking up the Democratic Party now when Roosevelt had made similar promises on civil rights. Thurmond replied, "But Truman really means it."

We affirm that a political party is an instrumentality for effectuating the principles upon which the party is founded; that a platform of principles is a solemn covenant with the people and with the members of the party; that no leader of the party, in temporary power, has the right or privilege to proceed contrary to the fundamental principles of the party, or the letter or spirit of the Constitution of the United States; that to act contrary to these principles is a breach of faith, a usurpation of power, and a forfeiture of the party name and party leadership.

We believe that the protection of the American people against the onward march of totalitarian government requires a faithful observance of Article X of the American Bill of Rights which provides that: "The powers not delegated to the United States by the Constitution, nor prohibited by it to the states, are reserved to the states respectively, or to the people."

The Principle of States' Rights

We direct attention to the fact that the first platform of the Democratic Party, adopted in 1840, resolved that: "Congress has no power under the Constitution to interfere with or control the domestic institutions of the several states, and that such states are the sole and proper judges of everything appertaining to their own affairs not prohibited by the Constitution."

Such pronouncement is the cornerstone of the Democratic Party. A long train of abuses and usurpations of power by unfaithful leaders who are alien to the Democratic parties of the states here represented has become intolerable to those who believe in the preservation of constitutional government and individual liberty in America.

The Executive Department of the government is promoting the gradual but certain growth of a totalitarian state by domination and control of a politically minded Supreme Court. As examples of the threat to our form of government, the Executive Department, with the aid of the Supreme Court, has asserted national dominion and control of submerged oil-bearing lands in California, schools in Oklahoma and Missouri, primary elections in Texas, South Carolina and Louisiana, restrictive covenants in New York and the District of Columbia, and other jurisdictions, as well as religious instruction in Illinois.

Peril to Basic Rights

By asserting paramount Federal rights in these instances, a totalitarian concept has been promulgated which threatens the integrity of the states and the basic rights of their citizens.

We have repeatedly remonstrated with the leaders of the national organization of our party but our petitions, entreaties and warnings have been treated with contempt. The latest response to our entreaties was a Democratic convention in Philadelphia rigged to embarrass and humiliate the South.

This alleged Democratic assembly called for a civil-rights law that would eliminate segregation of every kind from all American life, prohibit all forms of discrimination in private employment, in public and private instruction and administration and treatment of students; in the operation of public and private health facilities; in all transportation, and require equal access to all places of public accommodation for persons of all races, colors, creeds and national origin.

Proposed FBI Powers

This infamous and iniquitous program calls for the reorganization of the civil rights section of the Department of Justice with a substantial increase in a bureaucratic staff to be devoted exclusively to the enforcement of the civil rights program; the establishment within the FBI of a special unit of investigators and a police state in a totalitarian, centralized, bureaucratic government.

This convention hypocritically denounced totalitarianism abroad but unblushingly proposed and approved it at home. This convention would strengthen the grip of a police state upon a liberty-loving people by the imposition of penalties upon local public officers who failed or refused to act in accordance with its ideas in suppressing mob violence.

We point out that if a foreign power undertook to force upon the people of the United States the measures advocated by the Democratic convention in Philadelphia, with respect to civil rights, it would mean war and the entire nation would resist such effort.

The convention that insulted the South in the party platform advocated giving the Virgin Islands and other dependencies of the United States "the maximum degree of local self-government."

When an effort was made to amend this part of the platform so as to make it read that the party favored giving the Virgin Islands and the several states the maximum degree of local self-government, the amendment adding the words "these several states" was stricken out and the sovereign states were denied the rights that the party favors giving the Virgin Islands.

Past Loyalty

We point out that the South, with clock-like regularity, has furnished the Democratic Party approximately 50 per cent of the votes necessary to nominate a President every four years for nearly a century. In 1920 the only states in the union that went Democratic were the eleven Southern states.

Notwithstanding this rugged loyalty to the party, the masters of political intrigue now allow Republican states in which there is scarcely a Democratic office holder to dominate and control the party and fashion its policies.

New Policy

As Democrats who are irrevocably committed to democracy as defined and expounded by Thomas Jefferson, Andrew Jackson and Woodrow Wilson, and who believe that all necessary steps must be taken for its preservation, we declare to the people of the United States as follows:

1. We believe that the Constitution of the United States is the greatest charter of human liberty ever conceived by the mind of man.

2. We oppose all efforts to invade or destroy the rights vouchsafed by it to every citizen of this republic.

3. We stand for social and economic justice, which we believe can be vouchsafed to all citizens only by a strict adherence to our Constitution and the avoidance of any invasion or destruction of the constitutional rights of the states and individuals. We oppose the totalitarian, centralized, bureaucratic government and the police state called for by the platforms adopted by the Democratic and Republican conventions.

4. We stand for the segregation of the races and the racial integrity of each race; the constitutional right to choose one's associates; to accept private employment without governmental interference; and to earn one's living in any lawful way. We oppose the elimination of segregation employment by Federal bureaucrats called for by the misnamed civil rights program. We favor home rule, local self-government and a minimum interference with individual rights.

5. We oppose and condemn the action of the Democratic convention in sponsoring a civil rights program calling for the elimination of segregation, social equality by Federal fiat, regulation of private employment practices, voting and local law enforcement.

6. We affirm that the effective enforcement of such a program would be utterly destructive of the social, economic and political life of the Southern people, and of other localities in which there may be differences in race, creed or national origin in appreciable numbers.

7. We stand for the checks and balances provided by the three departments of our Government. We oppose the usurpation of legislative functions by the executive and judicial departments. We unreservedly condemn the effort to

> **When the ballots were counted, Truman had pulled off the greatest upset in U.S. political history, winning 24,105,695 popular votes and 303 electoral vote to Dewey's 21,069,170 and 189. Thurmond carried only four states in the Deep South and Wallace carried no states at all, although each received 2.4 percent of the popular vote. The Democrats recaptured control of both houses of Congress and also won 21 out of 33 contests for governor. Perhaps Truman's greatest achievement was winning without the assistance of the Solid South. Shortly after his dramatic election, Truman quipped, "I am just an ordinary human being who has been lucky."**

establish nation-wide a police state in this republic that would destroy the last vestige of liberty enjoyed by a citizen.

8. We demand that there be returned to the people, to whom of right they belong, those powers needed for the preservation of human rights and the discharge of our responsibility as Democrats for human welfare. We oppose a denial of those rights by political parties, a barter or sale of those rights by a political convention, as well as any invasion or violation of those rights by the Federal Government.

We call upon all Democrats and upon all other loyal Americans who are opposed to totalitarianism at home and abroad to unite with us in ignominiously defeating Harry S. Truman and Thomas E. Dewey, and every other candidate for public office who would establish a police state in the United States of America.

The Military Is Desegregated

Throughout World War II, the army (and the air force as a part of the army) followed a racial policy that restricted African Americans to 10 percent of enlisted strength, segregated units, and greatly limited job opportunities. The navy did not accept blacks in any capacity other than as mess attendants until 1943—at that time the War Manpower Commission ordered the navy to accept blacks in the same proportion as the other branches.

On July 26, 1948, Truman issued Executive Order 9835 (an executive order commands government officials to take or refrain from taking some kind of action). This order established a policy of "equality of treatment and opportunity for all persons in the armed forces without regard to race, color, religion, or national origin" and created a presidential committee to oversee its implementation.

Establishing the President's Committee on Equality of Treatment and Opportunity in the Armed Services

WHEREAS it is essential that there be maintained in the armed services of the United States the highest standards of democracy, with equality of treatment and opportunity for all those who serve in our country's defense:

NOW, THEREFORE, by virtue of the authority vested in me as President of the United States, by the Constitution and the statutes of the United States, and as Commander in Chief of the armed services, it is hereby ordered as follows:

1. It is hereby declared to be the policy of the President that there shall be equality of treatment and opportunity for all persons in the armed services without regard to race, color, religion, or national origin. This policy shall be put into effect as rapidly as possible, having due regard to the time required to effectuate any necessary changes without impairing efficiency or morale.

2. There shall be created in the National Military Establishment an advisory committee to be known as the President's Committee on Equality of Treatment and Opportunity in the Armed Services, which shall be composed of seven members to be designated by the President.

3. The Committee is authorized on behalf of the President to examine the rules, procedures and practices of the armed services in order to determine in what respect such rules, procedures, and practices may be altered or improved with a view to carrying out the policy of this order. The Committee shall confer and advise with the Secretary of Defense, the Secretary of the Army, the Secretary of the Navy, and the Secretary of the Air Force, and shall make such recommendations to the President and to said Secretaries as in the judgment of the Committee will effectuate the policy hereof.

4. All executive departments and agencies of the Federal Government are authorized and directed to cooperate with the Committee in its work, and to furnish the Committee such information or the services of such person as the Committee may require in the performance of its duties.

Selection of items from the 1948 campaign. The end of wartime shortages led to a revival in ephemera—buttons, ribbons, pennants, pencils, and all types of novelties.

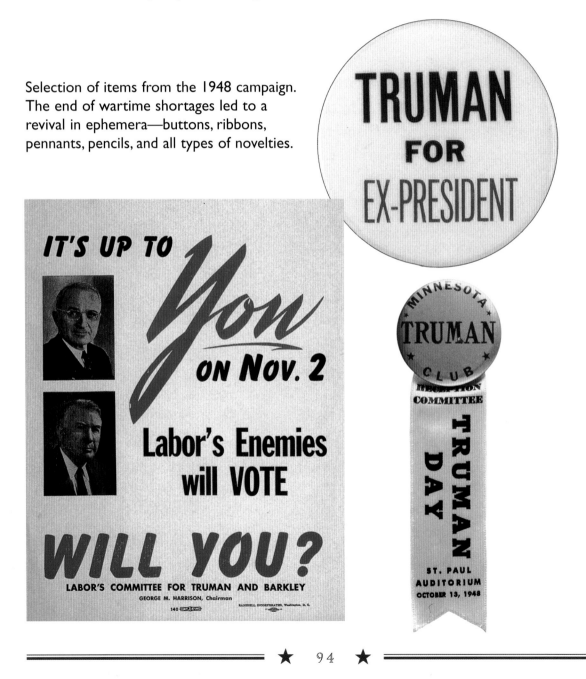

TRUMAN FOR EX-PRESIDENT

IT'S UP TO _You_ ON NOV. 2

Labor's Enemies will VOTE

WILL YOU?

LABOR'S COMMITTEE FOR TRUMAN AND BARKLEY

GEORGE M. HARRISON, Chairman

RANSDELL, INCORPORATED, Washington, D. C.

140

MINNESOTA TRUMAN CLUB

RECEPTION COMMITTEE

TRUMAN DAY

ST. PAUL AUDITORIUM OCTOBER 13, 1948

5. When requested by the Committee to do so, persons in the armed services or in any of the executive departments and agencies of the Federal Government shall testify before the Committee and shall make available for the use of the Committee such documents and other information as the Committee may require.

6. The Committee shall continue to exist until such time as the President shall terminate its existence by executive order.

★ Pollster Predicts Dewey Victory ★

Throughout the presidential campaign, pollsters remained convinced that Dewey would win the election. The final presidential election survey of the Gallup Poll gave Dewey 49.5 percent of the vote. He actually received 45.1 percent.

In 1948, public opinion polls were in their infancy. The ability to sample the adult population and to project these findings to the national population required refinement. For example, in 1948 polling stopped about two weeks prior to the election because of the time required to tabulate and analyze the sample. (Today, polling continues until the morning of Election Day.) In these final two weeks, Truman increased his stumping of the country by train. Greeted by impressive crowds that bolstered his confidence, Truman presented himself as a "common man" and a champion of the "people" against the "special interests."

Pollster Elmo Roper wrote this essay which appeared in the *New York Herald Tribune* on September 9, 1948, two months before the election.

Opponents of public-opinion surveying often question the social value or desirability of predicting Presidential elections. This happens to be a year in which I very largely agree with them.

I agree with them because of my own belief, drawn from the statistics so far gathered, that Thomas E. Dewey is almost as good as elected to the Presidency of the United States.

Of course, to be professionally careful, one must make the usual hedges. Some sort of political convulsion could upset the trend of statistics as it is visible now. If the Russians should involve themselves in an actual war with the United States before Nov. 2, public opinion might rally heavily toward the man who would be Commander in Chief of our military forces engaged in war. If Mr. Truman should pull a brilliant coup somewhere in his foreign or domestic policy, that also might improve his standing. And if Mr. Dewey should err grossly in his political conduct or one of his campaigners make a modern-day equivalent of a "Rum, Romanism and Rebellion" speech, perhaps he might lose his presently commanding lead. These or other unpredictable possibilities, can never be completely dismissed, but as a practical guide to politics in the year 1948 I think they can be largely disregarded. Mr. Truman's campaign is not likely to evoke any electoral miracles and Mr. Dewey is not rash. So this is not a hare-and-tortoise race, and neither is it a race between two closely matched thoroughbreds; it is a very ordinary horse race—a race in which one horse already has a commanding lead over the other horse. Neither Mr. Wallace nor Governor Thurmond can be seen without binoculars.

That being so, I can think of nothing duller or more intellectually barren than acting like a sports announcer who feels he must pretend he is witnessing a neck-and-neck race that will end in a photo finish or a dramatic upset for the favorite—and then finally have to announce that the horse which was eight lengths ahead at the turn is still eight lengths ahead. So as of this Sept. 9, my whole inclination is to predict the election of Thomas E. Dewey by a heavy margin and devote my time and efforts to other things. The scores of issues that confront the United States and the public's reaction to them strike me as providing much more interesting and vital material for investigation by public opinion research than the Presidential "race" between Mr. Dewey and Mr. Truman.

Here, for example, are the latest figures we have gathered in a field survey just completed for "Fortune":

If the election were being held today, which candidate for President do you think you'd vote for—Harry S. Truman, Thomas E. Dewey, Henry Wallace, Norman Thomas, Strom Thurmond or whom?

Truman	31.4 percent
Dewey	44.2 percent
Wallace	3.6 percent
Thomas	5 percent
Thurmond	4.4 percent
Other	5 percent
Don't know	15.4 percent

The most interesting thing about the figures in this table is that, so far as they can be compared, they bear an almost morbid resemblance to the Roosevelt-Landon figures as of about this time in 1936—except that this time the Republican candidate has the edge Mr. Roosevelt enjoyed in 1936, and the present President of the United States is the recipient of the acclaim poured out on Alf Landon twelve years ago. (This does not mean that my current statistics reveal the same figures as were computed in the 1936 election.)

In 1936, however, public-opinion testing in political areas was brand-new, and it had to be publicly validated. But we are now approaching the fourth

Presidential election since then and the validation is complete: it is known that a scientifically conducted and antiseptically clean survey will coincide with the actual choice of the voters within a close limit of error. If this were a year in which great men represented the great issues that face the world, I think it might be a vital matter to follow their destinies to the end. But this is not such a year. If Mr. Truman's popularity rises by 0.6 as the result of the speech he made on Labor Day, three days ago, I cannot see what it matters. If Mr. Dewey gains 2 more percentage points in October (or even loses them) this will not be news either.

I am not going to stop gathering facts about this Presidential election. But I am going to stop reporting on them unless something really interesting happens. My silence on this point can be construed as an indication that Mr. Dewey is still so clearly ahead that we might just as well get ready to listen to his inaugural on Jan. 20, 1949.

Since this is a somewhat unorthodox column in tone and content, I might just as well push unorthodoxy one step further and confess that, in general, I do not wholly approve of Presidential predicting under any circumstances. It has become a stunt. Like tearing a telephone directory in two, it impresses without instruction. Very different indeed from this stunting are the truly constructive uses of the public-opinion survey technique. To discover the opinions that people hold on vital questions; to try to get back of this to the difficult, and sometimes hazy reasons why they hold their opinions; to try to explain why Mr. Truman is in the fix; to discover areas of agreement and of ignorance and how they vary by geographical location, size of place, economic rank, professional status and all such matters—these things are to my belief, the things that make the surveying of public opinion a truly vital contribution to our knowledge of ourselves as groups and in the mass.

This generality has some bearing on my distaste for Presidential popularity contests. No one has yet solved the riddle of how, or why, or when a voter makes up his mind about a Presidential candidate. My own belief, however, is that the voter, no matter whether he is himself a political scientist or confused layman, somehow integrates in his own mind the salient events (to him) of the last four years—or three years or one year—of an administration, and then decides whether in his opinion the incumbent should be retained or thrown out. If I am right in this, then political campaigns are largely ritualistic: they are held because they have always been held, not because they decide or even heavily influence the election results. All the evidence that we have accumulated since 1936 tends to indicate that the man in the lead at the beginning of the campaign is the man who is the winner at the end of it. The closest election held since public opinion sampling began was the Roosevelt-Dewey campaign of 1944—and the results of this prove the contention as much as the 1936 campaign in which Roosevelt held a commanding lead from the beginning. The winner, it appears, clinches his victory early in the race and before he has uttered a word of campaign oratory. I should not be surprised to see Mr. Dewey, practiced campaigner that he is known to be, lose fractional percentages of his present margin as he successively discusses the myriads of topics from which he has hitherto held himself so skillfully aloof—yet not lose enough to lose the election or even come close to losing it. It was Mr. Truman who did that, sometime between the death of Mr. Roosevelt and the Democratic Convention of 1948, although there were times when it seemed that insurgent Democrats were more responsible for Mr. Truman's weakness than either Mr. Truman or the Republicans.

To be sure, a campaign may help to keep the doubtful supporters of each candidate in line. But the value of a Presidential campaign lies less with the impression it makes on the voters than the inspiration, if I may call it that, which it supplies to local politicians charged with getting out the vote. Since somebody always stands a chance of shoving himself up or of helping to elect others on his ticket, a campaign cannot be regarded as wholly useless.

This year, also, a number of important contests will occur for House and Senate seats and chairs in Governors' mansions. In writing off Mr. Truman's

Brochure for Dewey and Warren. While 65 percent of the nation's newspapers endorsed Dewey, only 15 percent favored Truman.

chances, I do not want to lead anyone to believe that the Republicans are going to sweep all, or even most, of these offices. There are several Democratic candidates for the Senate and the House and for Governorships who are going to run so far ahead of their ticket that Mr. Dewey's victory, resounding as it may be, probably won't cause their Republican opponents to win. We may even have a Democratic Senate.

There is a corollary to this whole business of prediction. The public-opinion analyst is often credited with a power which, in my opinion, he does not possess: the power to influence or lead what he thinks he is merely measuring. Any one holding that belief and reading this column may believe, if he is a "liberal," that my published opinion that Mr. Truman is fighting a hopeless fight for election will in itself contribute its mite to Mr. Truman's defeat and construe it as a stab in the back. If I held such a belief myself, it would be unlikely that I should write what I have written, except for another belief that the analyst has an obligation to report his findings and beliefs as soon as he acquires them, without regard for any personal feelings he may possess, and whether or not he agrees with the judgement of the majority.

Truman's Inaugural Address

"The oath-taking ceremony," wrote Harry Truman in his autobiography, "was scheduled for noon, but in the rotunda of the Capitol the gathering of diplomats, members of Congress, justices of the Supreme Court, and governmental officials was so great, and so many amenities had to be exchanged, that the signal for the Marine Band to play 'Hail to the Chief' was not actually given until twelve-fourteen. . . . The words were the same I had repeated three years and nine months earlier when I had been called so unexpectedly to the White House, but then only a handful of people were with me in the Cabinet Room. I raised my hand; once more I swore faithfully to defend the Constitution of the United States, repeating the short and simple oath, and kissed the Bible. Then I stepped to the rostrum to begin my inaugural address."

Mr. Vice President, Mr. Chief Justice, and fellow citizens, I accept with humility the honor which the American people have conferred upon me. I accept it with a deep resolve to do all that I can for the welfare of this Nation and for the peace of the world.

In performing the duties of my office, I need the help and prayers of every one of you. I ask for your encouragement and your support. The tasks we face are difficult, and we can accomplish them only if we work together.

Each period of our national history has had its special challenges. Those that confront us now are as momentous as any in the past. Today marks the beginning not only of a new administration, but of a period that will be eventful, perhaps decisive, for us and for the world.

It may be our lot to experience, and in large measure to bring about, a major turning point in the long history of the human race. The first half of this century has been marked by unprecedented and brutal attacks on the rights of man, and by the two most frightful wars in history. The supreme need of our time is for men to learn to live together in peace and harmony.

The peoples of the earth face the future with grave uncertainty, composed almost equally of great hopes and great fears. In this time of doubt, they look to the United States as never before for good will, strength, and wise leadership.

It is fitting, therefore, that we take this occasion to proclaim to the world the essential principles of the faith by which we live, and to declare our aims to all peoples.

The American people stand firm in the faith which has inspired this Nation from the beginning. We believe that all men have a right to equal justice under law and equal opportunity to share in the common good. We believe that all men have the right to freedom of thought and expression.

We believe that all men are created equal because they are created in the image of God.

From this faith we will not be moved.

The American people desire, and are determined to work for, a world in which all nations and all peoples are free to govern themselves as they see fit, and to achieve a decent and satisfying life. Above all else, our people desire, and are determined to work for, peace on earth—a just and lasting peace—based on genuine agreement freely arrived at by equals.

In the pursuit of these aims, the United States and other like-minded nations find themselves directly opposed by a regime with contrary aims and a totally different concept of life.

That regime adheres to a false philosophy which purports to offer freedom, security, and greater opportunity to mankind. Misled by this philosophy, many peoples have sacrificed their liberties only to learn to their sorrow that deceit and mockery, poverty and tyranny, are their reward.

That false philosophy is communism.

Communism is based on the belief that man is so weak and inadequate that he is unable to govern himself, and therefore requires the rule of strong masters.

Felt inaugural pennant with portrait of Truman. In addition to retaining the White House in 1948, Democrats regained control of Congress, securing a majority of 12 in the Senate and 93 in the House of Representatives.

Democracy is based on the conviction that man has the moral and intellectual capacity, as well as the inalienable right, to govern himself with reason and justice.

Communism subjects the individual to arrest without lawful cause, punishment without trial, and forced labor as the chattel of the state. It decrees what information he shall receive, what art he shall produce, what leaders he shall follow, and what thoughts he shall think.

Democracy maintains that government is established for the benefit of the individual, and is charged with the responsibility of protecting the rights of the individual and his freedom in the exercise of his abilities. Communism maintains that social wrongs can be corrected only by violence.

Democracy has proved that social justice can be achieved through peaceful change.

Communism holds that the world is so deeply divided into opposing classes that war is inevitable.

Democracy holds that free nations can settle differences justly and maintain lasting peace.

These differences between communism and democracy do not concern the United States alone. People everywhere are coming to realize that what is involved is material well-being, human dignity, and the right to believe in and worship God.

I state these differences, not to draw issues of belief as such, but because the actions resulting from the Communist philosophy are a threat to the efforts of free nations to bring about world recovery and lasting peace.

Since the end of hostilities, the United States has invested its substance and its energy in a great constructive effort to restore peace, stability, and freedom to the world.

We have sought no territory and we have imposed our will on none. We have asked for no privileges we would not extend to others.

We have constantly and vigorously supported the United Nations and related agencies as a means of applying democratic principles to international relations. We have consistently advocated and relied upon peaceful settlement of disputes among nations.

We have made every effort to secure agreement on effective international control of our most powerful weapon, and we have worked steadily for the limitation and control of all armaments.

We have encouraged, by precept and example, the expansion of world trade on a sound and fair basis.

Almost a year ago, in company with 16 free nations of Europe, we launched the greatest cooperative economic program in history. The purpose of that unprecedented effort is to invigorate and strengthen democracy in Europe, so that the free people of that continent can resume their rightful place in the forefront of civilization and can contribute once more to the security and welfare of the world.

Our efforts have brought new hope to all mankind. We have beaten back despair and defeatism. We have saved a number of countries from losing their liberty. Hundreds of millions of people all over the world now agree with us, that we need not have war—that we can have peace.

The initiative is ours.

We are moving on with other nations to build an even stronger structure of international order and justice. We shall have as our partners countries which, no longer solely concerned with the problem of national survival, are now working to improve the standards of living of all their people. We are ready to undertake new projects to strengthen the free world.

In the coming years, our program for peace and freedom will emphasize four major courses of action.

First, we will continue to give unfaltering support to the United Nations and related agencies, and we will continue to search for ways to strengthen their authority and increase their effectiveness. We believe that the United Nations will be strengthened by the new nations which are being formed in

lands now advancing toward self-government under democratic principles.

Second, we will continue our programs for world economic recovery.

This means, first of all, that we must keep our full weight behind the European recovery program. We are confident of the success of this major venture in world recovery. We believe that our partners in this effort will achieve the status of self-supporting nations once again.

In addition, we must carry out our plans for reducing the barriers to world trade and increasing its volume. Economic recovery and peace itself depend on increased world trade.

Third, we will strengthen freedom-loving nations against the dangers of aggression.

We are now working out with a number of countries a joint agreement designed to strengthen the security of the North Atlantic area. Such an agreement would take the form of a collective defense arrangement within the terms of the United Nations Charter.

We have already established such a defense pact for the Western Hemisphere by the treaty of Rio de Janeiro.

The primary purpose of these agreements is to provide unmistakable proof of the joint determination of the free countries to resist armed attack from any quarter. Each country participating in these arrangements must contribute all it can to the common defense.

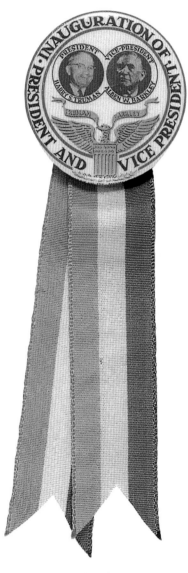

Celluloid badge from Truman's January 20, 1949, inauguration.

If we can make it sufficiently clear, in advance, that any armed attack affecting our national security would be met with overwhelming force, the armed attack might never occur.

I hope soon to send to the Senate a treaty respecting the North Atlantic security plan.

In addition, we will provide military advice and equipment to free nations which will cooperate with us in the maintenance of peace and security.

Fourth, we must embark on a bold new program for making the benefits of our scientific advances and industrial progress available for the improvement and growth of underdeveloped areas.

More than half the people of the world are living in conditions approaching misery. Their food is inadequate. They are victims of disease. Their economic life is primitive and stagnant. Their poverty is a handicap and a threat both to them and to more prosperous areas.

For the first time in history, humanity possesses the knowledge and the skill to relieve the suffering of these people.

The United States is pre-eminent among nations in the development of industrial and scientific techniques. The material resources which we can afford to use for the assistance of other peoples are limited. But our imponderable resources in technical knowledge are constantly growing and are inexhaustible.

I believe that we should make available to peace-loving peoples the benefits of our store of technical knowledge in order to help them realize their aspirations for a better life. And, in cooperation with other nations, we should foster capital investment in areas needing development.

Our aim should be to help the free peoples of the world, through their own efforts, to produce more food, more clothing, more materials for housing, and more mechanical power to lighten their burdens.

We invite other countries to pool their technological resources in this undertaking. Their contributions will be warmly welcomed. This should be a cooperative enterprise in which all nations work together through the United Nations and its specialized agencies wherever practicable. It must be a worldwide effort for the achievement of peace, plenty, and freedom.

With the cooperation of business, private capital, agriculture, and labor in this country, this program can greatly increase the industrial activity in other nations and can raise substantially their standards of living.

Such new economic developments must be devised and controlled to benefit the peoples of the areas in which they are established. Guarantees to the investor must be balanced by guarantees in the interest of the people whose resources and whose labor go into these developments.

The old imperialism—exploitation for foreign profit—has no place in our plans. What we envisage is a program of development based on the concepts of democratic fair-dealing.

All countries, including our own, will greatly benefit from a constructive program for the better use of the world's human and natural resources. Experience shows that our commerce with other countries expands as they progress industrially and economically.

Greater production is the key to prosperity and peace. And the key to greater production is a wider and more vigorous application of modern scientific and technical knowledge.

Only by helping the least fortunate of its members to help themselves can the human family achieve the decent, satisfying life that is the right of all people.

Special inaugural police badge from the District of Columbia Police Department.

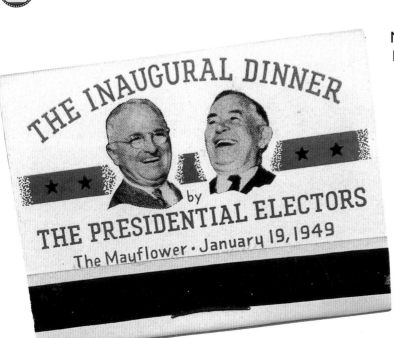

Matchbook from the 1949 inauguration.

Democracy alone can supply the vitalizing force to stir the peoples of the world into triumphant action, not only against their human oppressors, but also against their ancient enemies—hunger, misery, and despair.

On the basis of these four major courses of action we hope to help create the conditions that will lead eventually to personal freedom and happiness for all mankind.

If we are to be successful in carrying out these policies, it is clear that we must have continued prosperity in this country and we must keep ourselves strong.

Slowly but surely we are weaving a world fabric of international security and growing prosperity.

We are aided by all who wish to live in freedom from fear—even by those who live today in fear under their own governments.

We are aided by all who want relief from the lies of propaganda—who desire truth and sincerity.

We are aided by all who desire self-government and a voice in deciding their own affairs.

We are aided by all who long for economic security—for the security and abundance that men in free societies can enjoy.

We are aided by all who desire freedom of speech, freedom of religion, and freedom to live their own lives for useful ends.

Our allies are the millions who hunger and thirst after righteousness.

In due time, as our stability becomes manifest, as more and more nations come to know the benefits of democracy and to participate in growing abundance, I believe that those countries which now oppose us will abandon their delusions and join with the free nations of the world in a just settlement of international differences.

Events have brought our American democracy to new influence and new responsibilities. They will test our courage, our devotion to duty, and our concept of liberty.

But I say to all men, what we have achieved in liberty, we will surpass in greater liberty.

Steadfast in our faith in the Almighty, we will advance toward a world where man's freedom is secure.

To that end we will devote our strength, our resources, and our firmness of resolve. With God's help, the future of mankind will be assured in a world of justice, harmony, and peace.

Statement on Korea, June 26, 1950

The Cold War turned hot on June 25, 1950, 7,000 miles from the United States. Soldiers of the Communist-organized "People's Democratic Republic" of North Korea, using Russian-made tanks, drove across the 38th parallel into South Korea. Twenty-eight hours after the invasion, the United Nations Security Council ordered a cease-fire, which the Korean Communists ignored. Both the United States and the United Nations had assisted in establishing the South Korean Republic in 1947, and Marshall Plan aid and technical advice had been furnished to the young country. If the United States permitted South Korea to be overrun, would the Soviet Union incite a series of incursions in other parts of the world? Was this the ominous test to see if the democracies would resist Communist aggression?

President Truman issued this statement on June 26, 1950. The next day, Truman firmly announced his decision to send American air and sea forces into combat. The same day, an emergency session of the Security Council asked members to furnish armed forces to assist South Korea. On June 30, Truman ordered United States ground troops into action.

I conferred Sunday evening with the Secretaries of State and Defense, their senior advisors and the Joint Chiefs of Staff about the situation in the Far East created by unprovoked aggression against the Republic of Korea.

The government of the United States is pleased with the speed and determination with which the United Nations Security Council acted to order a withdrawal of the invading forces to positions north of the thirty-eighth parallel. In accordance with the resolution of the Security Council, the United States will vigorously support the effort of the Council to terminate this serious breach of the peace.

Our concern over the lawless action taken by the forces from North Korea, and our sympathy and support for the people of Korea in this situation, are being demonstrated by the cooperative action of American personnel in Korea, as well as by the steps taken to expedite and augment assistance of the type being furnished under the Mutual Defense Assistance Program.

Those responsible for this act of aggression must realize how seriously the government of the United States views such threats to the peace of the world. Willful disregard of the obligation to keep the peace cannot be tolerated by nations that support the United Nations Charter.

MacArthur Relieved of Command

The Korean War (1950–53) destroyed President Harry Truman's administration. The war had begun on June 25, 1950. After China entered the war on October 7, it became a stalemate. By mid-1952, the United States had suffered more than 100,000 casualties, including some 22,000 combat deaths. Republicans blamed Truman for having failed to define the "line of containment" against communist expansion.

In July 1950, General Douglas MacArthur took command of all UN troops in Korea. He reported to President Truman. A major disagreement developed on the conduct of the war—MacArthur wanted to bomb targets within China and Truman did not want to expand the war. In April 1951, MacArthur appealed to Congress over the President's authority. This was a deliberate challenge to the principle that the civilian power of the president must be stronger than the military. Truman felt he had no choice but to remove MacArthur from command. "I could do nothing else and still be President of the United States," wrote Truman.

With deep regret I have concluded that General of the Army Douglas MacArthur is unable to give his wholehearted support to the policies of the United States Government and of the United Nations in matters pertaining to his official duties. In view of the specific responsibilities imposed upon me by the Constitution of the United States and the added responsibility which has been entrusted to me by the United Nations, I have decided that I must make a change of command in the Far East. I have, therefore, relieved General MacArthur of his commands and have designated Lt. Gen. Matthew B. Ridgway as his successor.

Full and vigorous debate on matters of national policy is a vital element in the constitutional system of our free democracy. It is fundamental, however, that military commanders must be governed by the policies and directives issued to them in the manner provided by our laws and Constitution. In time of crisis, this consideration is particularly compelling.

General MacArthur's place in history as one of our greatest commanders is fully established. The nation owes him a debt of gratitude for the distinguished and exceptional service which he has rendered his country in posts of great responsibility. For that reason I repeat my regret at the necessity for the action I feel compelled to take in his case.

Court Ruling on Steel Mill Seizure

The case of *Youngstown Sheet & Tube Co. v. Sawyer* (1952) is one of the classic confrontations in American history between the president and the Supreme Court. During the Korean War, a labor dispute in the steel industry was referred to the Federal Wage Stabilization Board. The efforts of the board were unsuccessful, and a nationwide strike was threatened. Thereupon, President Truman directed the Secretary of Commerce to take over and operate the country's steel mills. No statute authorized this taking. The president claimed it was necessary to keep the steel mills functioning to avoid a national catastrophe because of the demands for steel caused by the war.

On June 2, 1952, the Supreme Court, in a majority opinion written by Justice Hugo Black, held that the seizure was illegal. In a scathing rebuke, Black reminded the president that the "Founders of this Nation entrusted the lawmaking power to the Congress alone in both good and bad times."

We are asked to decide whether the President [. . .] was acting within his constitutional power when he issued an order directing the Secretary of Commerce to take possession of and operate most of the Nation's steel mills. The mill owners argued that the President's order amounts to lawmaking, a legislative function which the Constitution has expressly confided to the Congress and not to the President. The Government's position is that the order was made on findings of the President that his action was necessary to avert a national catastrophe which would inevitably result from a stoppage of steel production, and that in meeting this grave emergency the President was acting within the aggregate of his constitutional powers as the Nation's Chief Executive and the Commander in Chief of the Armed Forces of the United States. [. . .]

The President's power, if any, to issue the order must stem either from an act of Congress or from the Constitution itself. There is no statute that expressly authorizes the President to take possession of property as he did here. Nor is there any act of Congress to which our attention has been directed from which such a power can fairly be implied. There are two statutes which do authorize the President to take both personal and real property under certain conditions. [. . .] However, the Government admits that these conditions were not met and that the President's order was not rooted in either of the statutes. [. . .]

Moreover, the use of the seizures technique to solve labor disputes in order to prevent work stoppages was not only unauthorized by any congressional enactment; prior to this controversy, Congress had refused to adopt that method of settling labor disputes. When the Taft-Hartley Act was under consideration in 1947, Congress rejected an amendment which would have authorized such governmental seizures in cases of emergency. Instead, the plan sought to bring about settlements by use of the customary devices of mediation, conciliation, investigations by boards of inquiry, and public reports. In some instances temporary injunctions were authorized to provide cooling-off periods. All this failing, unions were left free to strike. [. . .]

It is clear that if the president had authority to issue the order he did, it must be found in some provision of the Constitution. And it is not claimed that express constitutional language grants this power to the President. The contention is that presidential power should be implied from the aggregate of his powers under the Constitution. Particular reliance is placed on provisions in Article II which say that "The executive Power shall be vested in a President"; that "he shall take Care that the Laws be faithfully executed"; and that he "shall be Commander in Chief of the Army and Navy of the United States."

The order cannot properly be sustained as an exercise of the President's military power as Commander in Chief of the Armed Forces. The Government attempts to do so by citing a number of cases upholding broad powers in military commanders engaged in day-to-day fighting in a theater of war. Such cases need not concern us here. Even though "theater of war" be an expanding concept, we cannot with faithfulness to our constitutional system hold that the Commander in Chief of the Armed Forces has the ultimate power as such to take possession of private property in order to keep labor disputes from stopping production. This is a job for the Nation's lawmakers, not for its military authorities.

Nor can the seizure order be sustained because of the several constitutional provisions that grant executive power to the President. In the framework of our Constitution, the President's power to see that the laws are faithfully executed refutes the idea that he is to be a lawmaker. The Constitution limits his functions in the law-making process to the recommending of laws he thinks wise and the vetoing of laws he thinks bad. And the Constitution is neither silent nor equivocal about who shall make laws which the President is to execute. [. . .]

The President's order does not direct that a congressional policy be executed in a manner prescribed by Congress—it directs that a presidential policy be executed in a manner prescribed by the President. The preamble of the order itself, like that of many statutes, sets out reasons why the President believes certain policies should be adopted, proclaims these policies as rules of conduct to be followed, and again, like a statute, authorizes a government official to promulgate additional rules and regulations consistent with the policy proclaimed and needed to carry that policy into execution. The power of Congress to adopt such public policies as those proclaimed by the order is beyond question. It can authorize the taking of private property for public use. It can make laws regulating the relationships between employers and employees, prescribing rules designed to settle labor disputes, and fixing wages and working conditions in certain fields of our economy. The Constitution does not subject this lawmaking power of Congress to presidential or military supervision or control.

It is said that other Presidents without congressional authority have taken possession of private business enterprises in order to settle labor disputes. But even if this be true, Congress has not thereby lost its exclusive constitutional authority to make laws necessary and proper to carry out the powers vested by the Constitution "in the Government of the United States, or any Department or Officer thereof."

The Founders of this Nation entrusted the lawmaking power to the Congress alone in both good and bad times. It would do no good to recall the historical events, the fears of power and the hopes for freedom that lay behind their choice. Such a review would but confirm our holding that this seizure order cannot stand.

Truman's Farewell Address

In April 1952, President Truman announced that he would not be a candidate for the presidency in 1952. While he opposed a third term on principle, Truman also realized that he would face a most difficult re-election campaign. On January 19, 1953, Truman delivered this modest farewell address.

Truman returned to Independence, Missouri, where he wrote his memoirs and spoke out on public issues. He retained considerable moral influence within the Democratic Party. His standing as an effective, plain-speaking, straightforward leader grew steadily.

Good evening, my fellow Americans:

Next Tuesday, General Eisenhower will be inaugurated as President of the United States. I will be on a train on my way home to Independence, Missouri, to become a plain citizen. Inauguration Day will be a great demonstration of the democratic process. I am glad to be a part of the peaceful transfer of the vast power of the Presidency from my hands to his. There is no job like it on the face of the Earth. I want you all to realize how hard it is and to give Ike all the help he will need. The Cold War and the "hot war" in Korea will be great tests of his strength.

How will the Cold War end? It will end . . . someday . . . because of the great weakness of the Communist system. I have not a doubt in the world that a great change will occur. I have a deep and abiding faith in the destiny of free men. With strength and courage, we shall, someday, overcome.

When Franklin Roosevelt died, I thought there must be a million men more qualified than I to take up the Presidential task. But the work was mine to do. But always, I knew that I was not alone. I knew that you were working with me. And now, the time has come for me to say goodnight and God bless you all.

Further Reading

GENERAL REFERENCE

Israel, Fred L. *Student's Atlas of American Presidential Elections, 1789–1996.* Washington, D.C.: Congressional Quarterly Books, 1998.

Levy, Peter B., editor. *100 Key Documents in American History*. Westport, Conn.: Praeger, 1999.

Mieczkowski, Yarek. *The Routledge Historical Atlas of Presidential Elections.* New York: Routledge, 2001.

Polsby, Nelson W., and Aaron Wildavsky. *Presidential Elections: Strategies and Structures of American Politics*. 10th edition. New York: Chatham House, 2000.

Watts, J. F., and Fred L. Israel, editors. *Presidential Documents*. New York: Routledge, 2000.

Widmer, Ted. *The New York Times Campaigns: A Century of Presidential Races*. New York: DK Publishing, 2000.

POLITICAL AMERICANA REFERENCE

Cunningham, Noble E. Jr. *Popular Images of the Presidency: From Washington to Lincoln*. Columbia: University of Missouri Press, 1991.

Melder, Keith. *Hail to the Candidate: Presidential Campaigns from Banners to Broadcasts*. Washington, D.C.: Smithsonian Institution Press, 1992.

Schlesinger, Arthur M. jr., Fred L. Israel, and David J. Frent. *Running for President: The Candidates and their Images*. 2 vols. New York: Simon and Schuster, 1994.

Warda, Mark. *100 Years of Political Campaign Collectibles*. Clearwater, Fla.: Galt Press, 1996.

THE ELECTION OF 1948
and the Administration of Harry S. Truman

Bass, Jack, and Marilyn W. Thompson. *Ol' Strom: An Unauthorized Biography of Strom Thurmond*. Atlanta: Longstreet Press, 1998.

Donaldson, Gary A. *Truman Defeats Dewey*. Lexington: University Press of Kentucky, 1998.

Dulles, Allen W. *The Marshall Plan*. New York: Berg Publishing, 1993.

Gardner, Michael R. *Harry Truman and Civil Rights: Moral Courage and Political Risks*. Carbondale: Southern Illinois University Press, 2002.

Gullan, Harold I. *The Upset that Wasn't: Harry S. Truman and the Crucial Election of 1948*. Chicago: Ivan R. Dee, 1998.

Hogan, Michael J. *A Cross of Iron: Harry S. Truman and the Origins of the National Security State, 1945–1954*. London: Cambridge University Press, 1998.

Karabell, Zachary. *The Last Campaign: How Harry Truman Won the 1948 Election*. New York: Knopf, 2000.

McCullough, David. *Truman*. New York: Simon and Schuster, 1992.

Offner, Arnold A. *Another Such Victory: President Truman and the Cold War, 1945–1953*. Palo Alto, Calif.: Stanford University Press, 2002.

Schmidt, Karl M. *Henry A. Wallace: Quixotic Crusade in 1948*. Syracuse, N.Y.: Syracuse University Press, 1960.

INDEX

A

Albania, 50
Americans for Democratic Action (ADA), *81*
atomic bomb, 36, 44–47, 64, 69, 74
Attlee, Clement, 44
Austria, 59

B

Baldwin, Raymond E., 71
Barkley, Alben W., 23, 34, 76–77, 85
Beaucoup, Illinois, 29–30
Birmingham, Alabama, 86
Black, Hugo, 116
Blake, Eubie, *27*
Bulgaria, 50, 52
buttons. See memorabilia, political

C

campaigning, 8–14
    in 1948, 17–31, 33
    funding, 30–31
    and public opinion polls, 96–101
    "whistle-stop," 22–23, 24–25, *26*
Chicago Daily Tribune, 17, *32–33*
China, 36, 67, 79, 114
Churchill, Winston, 44, 46
civil rights, 24, 36, 83, 84
    as campaign issue, 20–21, 64–65, 76, *81*, 86,
        88, 90
Clifford, Clark, 18
    See also Clifford memorandum
Clifford memorandum, 18–20

See also campaigning
Cold War, 58, 112, 121
Columbia University, *81*
communism, 36, 48, 50, 68, 104–105, 112, 114,
    121
    See also Truman Doctrine
Congress, 67, *104*, 119
    and Douglas MacArthur, 114–115
    and Harry S. Truman, 17, 21–22, 26, 36, 54,
        56–57, 62, 76, 78–85
    and the New Deal, *53*
    and the Truman Doctrine, 48–49
Constitution, United States, 83, 87, 90, 115,
    117–119
    and political parties, 6–8

D

Democratic Party, *23*, 78–79, 86–87, *104*, 120
    and campaign funding, 30–31
    convention, 21–22, 64, 76–77, 88–90
    and the nomination of Harry S. Truman, 17
    and the Southern states, 89
    and third parties, 64, 65–66
    See also parties, political; Republican Party
desegregation, military, 92–95
    See also segregation
Dewey, Thomas E., 19, 91
    and the 1948 campaign, 17–18, 22–23, 26,
        27–30, 33, *37*, *82*
    memorabilia, *22*, *25*, *26*, *72*, *73*, *74*
    nomination acceptance speech of, 70–75
    victory of, predicted by polls, 96–101

Numbers in **bold italics** refer to captions.

Dexter, Iowa, 26, 29
Dixiecrats. See States' Rights Party
Douglas, William O., *81*

E

economic recovery, European, 58–62, 106–107
    See also Marshall Plan
education, 80–81
Eisenhower, Dwight D., 17, *74*, *81*, 121
election, presidential
    of 1936, 98
    of 1944, 100
    process of, 6, 15
    and public opinion polls, 17–18, 22, 33, 70,
        96–101
    votes (1948), 33, *37*, 62, 91
    See also campaigning
England. See Great Britain
Executive Order 9835 (military
    desegregation), 92–95

F

Fair Deal, *24*, 36
    See also Truman, Harry S.
farm prices, 19, 20, 78
Federal Bureau of Investigation (FBI), 88–89
Federal Wage Stabilization Board, 116
    See also strikes
foreign relations, 40–42, 48–52, 54–57, 67–69,
    78–79, 104–111
France, 68
funding, campaign, 30–31
    See also campaigning

G

Gallup polls. See polls, public opinion
Germany, 26–27, 40, 44–45, 49, 52, 59, 68
Great Britain, 46, 48, 51–52, 68–69
Greece, 36, 48–51, 52, 55–56, 67, 68, 79

H

Harvard University, 58
Hiroshima, 36, 44–45
Hitler, Adolf, 27, 40
Humphrey, Hubert, *81*

I

inaugural address, Harry S. Truman's, 102–111
Independence, Missouri, 120–121
inflation, 20, 54, 62, 65, 67, 84
Israel, 36
Italy, 37

J

Jackson, Andrew, 9, 10, 89
Japan, 36, 40, 41, 44–45, 46–47, 52
Jefferson, Thomas, 12, 66, 89
Johnson, Lyndon B., *19*, 21, *74*

K

Kansas City, Missouri, 34
Kennedy, John F., *74*
Korean War, 114, 116, 121

L

labor, 78, 80
    unions, 19, 36, 54, 62, 67
    See also strikes
Labor-Management Relations Act of 1947, 36,
    62
LaGuardia, Fiorello, 66
Lamar, Missouri, 34
Landon, Alf, 98
League of Nations. See United Nations
Lincoln, Abraham, 10, 11, 15, 66
Luce, Clare Boothe, 70

M

MacArthur, Douglas, 36, 71, 114–115
Marshall, George C., 35, 58
    See also Marshall Plan
Marshall Plan, 36, 58–63, 64, 68, 112
McGrath, J. Howard, 31
media, role of
    in elections, 12–13
memorabilia, political, *18, 20, 23, 28, 30, 67,*
    82, 94, 101, 104, 109, 110
        Harry S. Truman, *24, 27, 29, 53, 61, 107*
        Thomas E. Dewey, *22, 25, 26, 72, 73, 74*
Middle East, 52, 55
minimum wage, 20, 80, 84

N

Nagasaki, 36, 44
New Deal, *53, 81, 82*
New York City, New York, 31
New York Herald Tribune, 96
New York Times, 27, 76
newspapers. See press
Newsweek, 70
Norris, George, 66
North Atlantic Treaty Organization (NATO), 36, 107–108
North Korea, 36, 112–113

P

parties, political
    and campaigning, 11–13, 23, 25–26, 30–31, *82*
    growth of, 6–9
    platforms of, 9, 10
    third, 64, 65, 68
    See also Democratic Party; Republican Party
Pearl Harbor, 45
People's Democratic Republic of North Korea. See North Korea
Philadelphia, Pennsylvania, 70, 75, 76, 80, 88–89
platforms, political party, 9, 10
Poland, 52
polls, public opinion, 17–18, 22, 33, 70
    predict Dewey victory, 96–101
President, United States
    role of, 6–7, 13–14, 87–88, 116–119
press, 17, 22–23, 27, 31, *32*, 33, *101*
Progressive Party, 18, 31, *37*, 64, 68
    See also parties, political; Wallace, Henry A.
Puerto Rico, 36

R

radio, 20, 22–23, 30–31, 64
rallies, political, 22–23, 31, 33
Republican Party, 66
    and campaign funding, 30
    convention, 70–71
    and the Eightieth Congress, 22, 26, 27, 54, 62, 76, 78–85
    platform (1948), 72, 83–85
    See also Democratic Party; parties, political

Ridgway, Matthew B., 115
Roosevelt, Franklin D., 46, *61, 67*, 70, 78, 85, 86, 98
    death of, 36, 37, 38–39, 121
Roper, Elmo, 96
    See also polls, public opinion
Rowe, James, 18–19
Rumania, 52
Russia. See Soviet Union

S

Sawyer, Charles, 35, 36
segregation, 64–65, *81*, 86, 88, 90
    in the military, 92–95
    See also States' Rights Party
separation of powers, 7–8, 87–88, 90–91, 116–119
    See also Constitution, United States
shortages, 54
    European postwar, 58–60
Social Security, 20, 81–82, 84
South Korean Republic, 112–113
Soviet Union, 58, 64, 68–69, 97, 112
special interests, 77, 96
speeches, 11, 14, 23–24, 28, 29
    Dewey's nomination acceptance, 70–75
    George C. Marshall's, on the Marshall Plan, 58–63
    Henry A. Wallace's candidacy announcement, 64–69
    inaugural address (Truman's), 102–111
    radio, 22–23
    Truman's, after Roosevelt's death, 38–43
    Truman's farewell address, 120–121
    Truman's nomination acceptance, 76–85
Stalin, Joseph, 44
Stassen, Harold E., 71
State of the Union address, 20–21, 36, 79
states' rights, 88, 90
States' Rights Party, 18, *21, 37*, 64, *81*
    platform, 86–91
strikes, 36, 54
    steel mill, 116–119
    See also labor
Supreme Court, United States, 36, *74*, 87–88
    and steel mill strikes, 116–119

T

Taft, Robert A., 71
Taft-Hartley Bill, 36, 62, 80, 117
television, 22, 31
Thomas, Norman, 98
Thurmond, J. Strom, 18, 21, 33, 37, 64, 86, 91,
    97, 98
Time, 70
Truman, Elizabeth "Bess" (Mrs. Harry S.
    Truman), 34
Truman, Harry S., *20*, 36, 91
    and the 1948 campaign, 17–22, 23–27, 28,
        31, 33, *37*, 62, 64, 70, *82*, 86
    and the atomic bomb, 44–47
    and Douglas MacArthur, 114–115
    facts at a glance, 34–37
    farewell address of, 120–121
    inaugural address of, 102–111
    and Korea, 112–115
    and the Marshall Plan, 58
    memorabilia, *24, 27, 29, 53, 61, 107*
    and military desegregation (Executive
        Order 9835), 92–95
    nomination acceptance speech of, 76–85
    political positions of, 34
    and public opinion polls, 96–97, 99, 100
    speech to Congress after Roosevelt's
        death, 38–43
    and steel mill strikes, 116
    and the Truman Doctrine, 36, 48–52, 54–57
Truman Committee, 38
    See also Truman, Harry S.
Truman Doctrine, 36, 48–52, 54–57, 68
Turkey, 36, 48–49, 51–52, 55–56, 67, 79

U

unemployment compensation, 20
unions, labor, 19, 36, 54, 62, 67
    See also labor; strikes
United Nations, 36, 43, 50, 52, 55, 68–69, 78,
    105–107, 109
    and Korea, 112–113, 114–115
University of Kansas City Law School, 34

V

Vandenberg, Arthur, 71
Virgin Islands, 89

W

Wagner-Ellender-Taft Bill, 80
Wallace, Elizabeth (Mrs. Harry S. Truman), 34
Wallace, Henry A., 18, 19, *20*, 23, 33, 35, *37*,
    81, 82, 91, 97, 98
        candidacy announcement of, 64–69
War Manpower Commission, 92
    See also desegregation, military
war profiteering, 38
Warren, Earl, 23, 70–71, *72, 74*
Warren Commission, *74*
    See also Warren, Earl
welfare state, 21, 53
Willkie, Wendell, 66
Wilson, Woodrow, 12, 78, 89
World War I, 58
World War II, 36, 38, 40–42, 44–47, 52, 54, 56,
    92
Wright, Fielding, *21*, 86

Y

Yalta Agreement, 52
Youngstown Sheet & Tube Co. v. Sawyer, 116–119
    See also strikes
Yugoslavia, 50

The EDITORS

ARTHUR M. SCHLESINGER JR. holds the Albert Schweitzer Chair in the Humanities at the Graduate Center of the City University of New York. He is the author of more than a dozen books, including *The Age of Jackson; The Vital Center; The Age of Roosevelt* (3 vols.); *A Thousand Days: John F. Kennedy in the White House; Robert Kennedy and His Times; The Cycles of American History;* and *The Imperial Presidency.* Professor Schlesinger served as Special Assistant to President Kennedy (1961–63). His numerous awards include: the Pulitzer Prize for History; the Pulitzer Prize for Biography; two National Book Awards; The Bancroft Prize; and the American Academy of Arts and Letters Gold Medal for History.

FRED L. ISRAEL is professor emeritus of American history, City College of New York. He is the author of *Nevada's Key Pittman* and has edited *The War Diary of Breckinridge Long* and *Major Peace Treaties of Modern History, 1648–1975* (5 vols.) He holds the Scribe's Award from the American Bar Association for his joint editorship of the *Justices of the United States Supreme Court* (4 vols.). For more than 25 years Professor Israel has compiled and edited the Gallup Poll into annual reference volumes.

DAVID J. FRENT is the president of Political Americana Auctions, Oakhurst, NJ. With his wife, Janice, he has assembled the nation's foremost private collection of political campaign memorabilia. Mr. Frent has designed exhibits for corporations, the Smithsonian Institution, and the United States Information Agency. A member of the board of directors of the American Political Items Collectors since 1972, he was elected to its Hall of Fame for his "outstanding contribution to preserving and studying our political heritage."